# MIND MAPPING

A Guide to Improve Concentration, Memory and Creativity

(Business and Marketing Planning)

**Renee Graves**

Published by Sharon Lohan

© **Renee Graves**

All Rights Reserved

*Mind Mapping: A Guide to Improve Concentration, Memory and Creativity (Business and Marketing Planning)*

ISBN 978-1-990334-60-3

All rights reserved. No part of this guide may be reproduced in any form without permission in writing from the publisher except in the case of brief quotations embodied in critical articles or reviews.

Legal & Disclaimer

The information contained in this book is not designed to replace or take the place of any form of medicine or professional medical advice. The information in this book has been provided for educational and entertainment purposes only.

The information contained in this book has been compiled from sources deemed reliable, and it is accurate to the best of the Author's knowledge; however, the Author cannot guarantee its accuracy and validity and cannot be held liable for any errors or omissions. Changes are periodically made to this book. You must consult your doctor or get professional medical advice before using any of the suggested remedies, techniques, or information in this book.

Upon using the information contained in this book, you agree to hold harmless the Author from and against any damages, costs, and expenses, including any legal fees potentially resulting from the application of any of the information provided by this guide. This disclaimer applies to any damages or injury caused by the use and application, whether directly or indirectly, of any advice or information presented, whether for breach of contract, tort, negligence, personal injury, criminal intent, or under any other cause of action.

You agree to accept all risks of using the information presented inside this book. You need to consult a professional medical practitioner in order to ensure you are both able and healthy enough to participate in this program.

# Table of Contents

INTRODUCTION .................................................................. 1

CHAPTER 1 - FIND A WAY TO REMEMBER YOUR IDEAS ..... 3

CHAPTER 2: THE BENEFITS OF USING MIND MAPS ............ 7

CHAPTER 3: TECHNIQUES USED IN MIND MAPPING ........ 13

CHAPTER 4: ELEMENTS OF A MIND MAP .......................... 32

CHAPTER 5: BENEFITS OF MIND MAPPING ....................... 44

CHAPTER 6: BENEFITS OF MIND MAPPING ....................... 51

CHAPTER 7: EDUCATIONAL MIND MAPPING .................... 64

CHAPTER 8: MAKE THE RIGHT DECISIONS ........................ 80

CHAPTER 9: SECRETS ON CREATING YOUR OWN MIND MAPS .......................................................................................... 97

CHAPTER 10: LATERAL THINKING AND LINEAR THINKING .................................................................................................. 105

CHAPTER 11: KNOW WHAT TYPE OF WRITING YOU ARE GOING TO DO AND WHO YOU ARE WRITING FOR ......... 113

CHAPTER 12: IMPROVE YOUR MEMORY WITH MIND MAPPING ................................................................................. 118

CHAPTER 13: EXAMPLES OF MIND MAPPING AND MIND MAPPING SOFTWARE ........................................................... 122

CHAPTER 14: POTENTIAL USES OF MIND MAP ............... 142

CHAPTER 15: HOW TO INCREASE MEMORY CAPACITY .. 170

**CHAPTER 16: GOAL SETTING AND PLANNING WITH MIND MAPS .......................................................... 178**

**CHAPTER 17: THE BENEFITS OF USING MIND MAPS ...... 183**

**CHAPTER 18: LISTENING SKILLS AND MIND MAPPING... 189**

**CONCLUSION................................................................ 194**

## Introduction

Mind mapping is a visual depiction of ordered data/information/facts that consists of a crucial or main idea surrounded by attached "roads" of associated topics. Your mind map can be constructed on paper using pencil or pen and colored markers or on a computer using a specifically designed program for mind mapping. The majority of mind maps contain both graphics or small pictures and words or keywords to help the process of learning and ordering.

A mind map could be used for everything from organizing business proposals to setting up a child's household chores for their weekly allowance. Mind maps are helpful for organizing, learning, problem solving and presenting large or small amounts of information or data so that nothing is forgotten and it is arranged in a more coherent manor.

I've written this book to explore the subject of mind mapping and how this can help you improve your memory, hone in your critical thinking and of course increase your learning efficiency.

I'll first of all explore the basics to bring you up to speed and then move onto the advanced techniques. Upon finishing this book you'll obtain skills that will help you become smarter and more efficient in learning.

Remember learning is an art and when you utilise the your brain to its full potential you will be able to achieve far greater feats, build more confidence and develop yourself far better than the average individual.

# Chapter 1 - Find A Way To Remember Your Ideas

This step is very crucial to achieving your goals because organizing your thoughts will be impossible if you can't even remember the things that you thought about. Everything you think about will somehow be stored in your brain. However that does not mean that they will be easy to remember especially if you do not do things to make sure you remember. Some information will be stored in your short term memory and some in your long term memory. The things you do to remember the information will then greatly affect where these information are stored. Perhaps you could try playing memory games or brain teasers if you enjoy playing those kinds of games.

Tip 1: Write Down Your Thoughts and Ideas

With the rise of technology and the advancement of technology writing using a pen and paper is slowly becoming a dying art. People these days prefer to take note of things using gadgets. However studies show that writing things down increases the chances of remembering things as compared to taking note using a gadget. One of the reasons behind this is the fact that when you write things down you only focus on that task and it allows that thought to be placed in your long term memory rather than in your short term memory.

Tip 2: Make Visual Representations or Aids

Having a physical reminder of your thoughts and ideas can also help you remember them. Although it was mentioned that writing information down is better than simply looking and memorizing, that technique does not guarantee that you will remember 100% of things your brain processes. With that said it is important to have physical reminders as a backup. Some of these could be simple things like post it notes or pictures. There is a saying "A picture is worth a thousand words." When you associate and idea to an image it will be helpful in remembering that idea. Try it out, you'll see!

Tip 3: Share Your Ideas to Other People

Constantly trying to remember your ideas is also a good way to remember them. They get imprinted in your memory more often and therefore better. One way of doing this is by sharing your ideas to other people. There are many ways to do this especially with the help of technology. The simplest way is by talking about it with your friends or family. Using technology you can blog about your ideas or post them on social media sites such as Facebook or Twitter. You never know, someone might even like your ideas and help you achieve them.

Tip 4: Do Not Destroy Your Brain Cells

As mentioned earlier the brain is key to organizing your thoughts. It is where all the information you want to remember is stored. Therefore keeping your brain healthy is also important. One of the simplest ways is to stay away from stress. Refrain from going near stressful environments and doing stressful jobs. Also find ways to release stress. Another way is to eat the right things. Look for food that is rich in Vitamin A, B and D and also rich in Selenium. All of these will help protect your brain and ensure better functioning. Besides it will also do your body good to eat healthier.

# Chapter 2: The Benefits Of Using

## Mind maps

There are a lot of benefits in using mind maps, no matter where you are in your life or what you do. They are a powerful tool that anyone can tap into and use for their benefit.

Perhaps the biggest benefit of mind maps is that they literally map the way your brain sees the universe around you and create connections between disparate items. Mind maps help to bring clarity to any learning or decision making process, combining the different functions your brain uses to process information.

When you are mind-mapping, you are using your whole brain to think.

The benefit of a mind map is that you can very quickly, and easily see which are the most important ideas by how close they are to the concept at the centre and by how it's represented.

The links between concepts can be seen at a glance, allowing your brain to form connections between the different concepts. This helps you review and learn the concepts and their connections very quickly as your brain can recall and visualize it very easily.

A mind map is also very easy to expand upon. You can easily add in more information and concepts as you learn more about the subject. They aren't static at all, being a dynamic form of representing the information you wish to record.

Mind maps form patterns with shapes and colors, which are something your brain is very good at remembering. Even just visualizing the pattern of your mind map can assist with recall of the information. This visualization helps your brain make connections between the different concepts and different pieces of information that you have recorded, helping you to piece together this information and make leaps of knowledge.

Mind maps have a lot of benefits, even more than the above. As said previously, they are powerful tools that can help you grasp concepts, make decisions and learn information in a much faster and simpler way than traditional methods. Some of the areas mind maps can benefit you in are:

**Learning:** Mind maps help you to feel good about studying and revising. They are excellent in helping boost your confidence in your ability to learn and to study for exams.

**Overviewing:** When learning or problem solving, being able to take a bird's eye view of the issues at hand can be very helpful. Mind maps help you to understand the links and connections between the different issues, allowing you to make connections you may not have otherwise made.

**Concentration:** Mind maps help you to focus on the tasks at hands and use all your mental abilities to focus your attention. The mind map itself is designed to attract your attention and to aid in concentration.

**Memorizing:** Using a visual medium helps you to memorize, as most people respond well to visual stimuli. You can 'see' your mind map in your mind's eye, which helps with recall.

**Organization:** Mind maps are an excellent way for you to organize information for projects and revision, amongst other things.

**Presentations:** You can use mind maps to help you give a presentation and keep on track and focused on the information you want to present to your audience.

**Brainstorming:** Mind maps are an excellent medium for brainstorming and will allow you to organize your thoughts and ideas in a coherent manner that makes sense after the session has finished.

**Problem Solving:** If you have a problem then you can present all the information in the form of a mind map and use this to connect the dots between pieces of information. This will allow you to creatively solve problems and find solutions you may not have otherwise seen.

**Thinking:** Sometimes you just need to have clarity of thought, and a mind map is an excellent medium for this. You can use mind maps to map out your thoughts and feelings on any subject.

**Summarizing Books/Seminars:** A lot of people like to summarize books or seminars and mind maps are an excellent way to do this. You can summarize the information concisely and relate points and ideas to each other.

**Planning:** Use mind maps to help you plan a project or event. They can clearly present information and be used to ensure that all processes and eventualities are captured.

There are a lot of benefits for using mind maps in your career and in your personal life. There are millions of people across the world that regularly use mind maps and benefit from them. You too can reap the benefits of this powerful technique to help you study better, work smarter and succeed in your life.

# Chapter 3: Techniques Used in Mind Mapping

After reading the various applications of mind mapping, I bet you are curious to learn some techniques. Basically, mind mapping just like any reading technique that uses visualization is a method that utilizes images and diagrams to make learning effective and comprehension easier. The truth is that mind mapping is a relatively easy note-making tool that involves limited resources. Essentially, all you need is a blank unlined paper, some colored pencils and pens, your brain and your imagination! When you start using mind mapping, you will quickly figure out that life can be much more productive, successful and fulfilled. It is amazing how much connections and ideas your brain can accommodate at any given time. There is no limit as to the number of applications you can use mind maps to help you.

## 1. Mind Mapping and Brainstorming

Brainstorming is a brilliant way of coming up with new ideas and solving problems. It enables you to evaluate the problems from a different perspective, understand the challenges and their root causes, and identify alternative solutions. You can also use brainstorming for decision-making and impact analysis. In the context of project management, you can brainstorm from the goals and objectives, down to the projects to explore new alternatives, ideas, and possibilities. It provides you with a much more complete and understandable plan than the task level planning.

Brainstorming can be particularly great for team building, which involves shared discussions, as well as for individual ideation. It also has the benefit of improving innovation and initiative with an organization, as well as improving profitability and quality, morale and efficiency.

## Basic Concepts of Brainstorming

Basically, brainstorming involves capturing ideas as quickly as possible in order to bypass the judgment you usually use to assess ideas before you record them and, instead, capture the ideas as they come up, assuming no time, resource, money, or other constraints, without judgment, and build on ideas as they occur as well as pushing yourself to think in new perspectives. The idea is that quality comes out of quantity. There are bound to be great ideas from the pile of ideas you throw in. You should be recording the keywords on topics as you come up with the ideas. When doing this, you don't particularly pay attention to where the topic ends up. However, as long as it is not slowing you down, you can as well group the main topics together and incorporate related ideas as subtopics. Sometimes it can be useful to have some high-end grouping by placing some of the main topics in their place and float the topics under your main ideas, creating islands of information that you can refine and organize later on. To help you keep up with the recording, you can simply type the topic, finish by pressing Return/Finish, and then create the next topic by pressing Return/Enter, and so forth. This way, recording the information will be fast as the details come up.

What If You Run out of Ideas?

Sometimes when brainstorming, you may run out of ideas and are stuck completely, or you may find that there are more ideas related to the main topic than you are already aware of.

For starters, if you are convinced that there should be more ideas linked to a certain topic, or extra concepts to be derived from the title, include blank topics in your Mind Map, as your subconscious mind does not like to leave things hanging, and will explore new ideas to fill the blank topics.

On the other hand, you can stop what you are doing and take a break by doing something else, or going for a walk. Engaging in a different activity enables your subconscious mind to work on the problem and identify new answers without being under too much pressure. Repetitive activities such as walking are especially great for allowing the thoughts to surface. Changing the scenery like walking by the beach or going to the park can result in a different kind of inspiration where you can think of different ideas. You can decide to take your laptop with you or something that will enable you to record the ideas as they spring to mind instead of holding them in your mind until you get to the office.

In most cases, when you are thinking about a certain topic, it is not uncommon to be stuck in a loop, where it seems like there is a truck parked in front of the road, and it is very difficult to think of new ideas. This is where it can help to introduce random ideas and words to jolt your memory. It can be helpful to use a thesaurus first to find related words and then move progressively away from your starting point. At a suitable point, you can then stop and identify the associations back to the initial concept. In some cases, it can be more thrilling to pick a random word from the website or dictionary, and then try relating it to the topic at hand.

Another idea is looking at similar problems in various domains and determining whether you can apply similar solutions that worked in the related domain. It can also help to ask yourself how other people would approach or solve the problem. This is especially useful when taking other parties' perspectives that are involved in the problem or are affected by the solution. Some questions you can ask include

- Who?

- What?

- How?

- When?

- Why?

- Who does this affect?

- How often?

These questions will encourage you to look at the problem from a different point of view. This idea is based on neurolinguistics and involves putting your imagination into play. It is like acknowledging that there is no other option but assuming that there was another option just for the meantime, what would it be? And in most cases, your imagination comes into play and provides another idea, and once again, the door that was shutting off ideas opens up.

Once you have recorded enough ideas, you have to organize so that you end up with the general concepts first, followed by the subtopics floating under the main ideas. This will help you see the bigger picture and the associated details. It is often useful to fix associated topics into floating groups and then incorporate the floating topic into the mind map. Ensure that the important ideas are highlighted with images or adornments or by color and so on.

Tips and Techniques

Let explore some important points for brainstorming both by yourself and in a group. The most important thing to do first is to define the topic or problem clearly. The subject should be the title of the mind map, and then imagine that you are getting your solutions and ideas from your inner advisor. Start with the top-level topics, followed by the children topics, or floating topics, as needed, without limitation or judgment, and not being concerned about organization. Stop when you have exhausted the ideas, or you have run out of ideas. Once you have enough ideas, you can then organize and evaluate them. Sometimes, you might have to expound the best ideas in the process in order to get more concrete detail.

When you are using mind maps in a group, you need some methods and structures in place to ensure the whole process goes smoothly. There should be a session leader, a recorder, and everyone else as the panel. It is generally not advisable to have a huge group. Having a group of more than ten to fifteen people can be hard to manage. In this case, it might be convenient splitting into several groups, and then incorporate the ideas later on, or reflect on the different aspects of the topic.

Studies have shown that if you start brainstorming with the whole group without first engaging in individual brainstorming, you usually end up with lower quality and fewer ideas. As such, begin by going through the topic identification and the intended purpose with the parties involved to ensure that you are on the same page. Proceed to brainstorm individually before getting back to share the ideas, ensuring that everyone gets a fair say. As you mention and record the ideas on the mind map, the ideas related to those topics will come up from the other participants, and these should be put down without constraints or judgment or elaboration. The point here is to simply get the keywords. The process of elaboration, culling, and grouping is pretty much the same as individual brainstorming. Using these techniques, and with this structure in place, you can brainstorm solutions and ideas either in a group or individually, and come up with better ideas and solutions.

Mind mapping is one of the best ways to brainstorm ideas and to arrange the ideas into sensible concepts. A great way to start is to dump your thoughts in a map and then let your imagination run wild as you continue to fill your mind map. Unfortunately, most people who use this technique when brainstorming use it wrongly. Here is how you can use mind maps effectively to brainstorm.

Generally, brainstorming has two phases: divergent thinking and convergent thinking. One common mistake people make while brainstorming is to start with convergent thinking.

The Two Stages of Brainstorming

Before you can develop the ability to create a mind map successfully, it is important to be conversant with the basics. Only then will you be able to use mind maps to brainstorm. The good news is that the process is relatively easy and quite effective.

You need to be aware of the two phases of brainstorming in order to get the most out of these sessions. During the first phase, you and the group generally come up with the topics and ideas you want to cover. This phase is also called divergent thinking. During this stage, you let the ideas flow freely, not thinking about the good and bad stuff, or the semantically correct. At that time, there are no connections or relationships between your thoughts. All the ideas and thoughts are just there as you dump them without judgment. You are basically thinking outside the box at this time, and you are not restricted to a framework or set of rules. It is like being a little child who does not understand how the world functions. The child will do whatever they think without being limited to anything, and this is exactly the state you want to be in while brainstorming. Convergent thinking is the second phase of brainstorming. At this stage, there is a set of rules governing your options as you try to get the best solution from what you have. This phase is particularly different from divergent thinking where you are allowed to think out of the box. Here, you start organizing your thoughts, map them, and then work on finding a solution from the available tangibles. If you relate it to the child analogy at this stage, you have grown up into an adult, you know the rules, and now you want to play under the confines of a set of rules and regulations. If you want to remember this easily, think of the first stage as a matter of quantity over quality; pour out all your thoughts, and then represent them using a mind map. Think of the second stage as a matter of quality over quantity. At this stage, you deal with the created thoughts and ideas from the first stage, sieve the thoughts you perceive irrelevant, and then organize the remaining information into finding a suitable solution.

2. Mind Mapping and Note-Taking

Picture this scenario: You go into your class as usual and find your lecturer just about to start, so you settle at your desk. As soon as the lecture begins, your mind wanders off, only to recover in the middle of the lesson without a clear view of how everything fits together.

This happens to everyone, and in most cases, it is caused by a lack of effective study skills that makes us lose concentration and end up assimilating much less information than our brains are capable. This is where you can use mind mapping. Mind mapping is an effective technique that improves your learning ability, enhances your method of recording information, and improves and supports creative problem-solving. You can easily identify and comprehend the structure of a topic with the help of mind maps. It becomes easy to see how all the pieces of information fit together. In addition, mind maps can also help you remember details since they record the information in your brain in a format that can be easily recalled by your mind. Here are a few tips to use when making notes:

Be Prepared

The first thing you need to do when taking notes is to be fully prepared. If you skip this step, you may end up losing plenty of information that you would have gained. To start, prepare a mind map with all the information you are already familiar with about the topic. Your mind works by linking new information to the old or existing information. As such, this forms a framework that can be added new information. Expand the mind map by incorporating new topics for the stuff you think or know may be covered. This creates the foundation of concentration for the new information. When this has been achieved, add branches for the topics you want to learn. This will help your mind look out for that information, helping you ask the relevant questions, both to the teacher and to yourself when you are listening to the presentation.

Color-Coding

Various topic shapes can be color-coded to represent the various topics. Different software allows you to choose colors that not only rhyme together but also have brilliant contrast. With these, you can easily color code stuff, as well as have a colorful mind map. One good approach is to set up these topics, and then let the subtopics take up these colors. At the end of the presentation, you can then easily identify the information you were already familiar with at a glance, the information you were expecting and received, and lastly, the answers to your questions.

Taking Notes Effectively

When in a study session, it is always advisable to add new topics for your existing topics as you learn some new and interesting information. If you can add the topics quickly on the map and position them where they belong, go ahead and do so. However, if you do not have the time for that, do not stress it.

How to Memorize the Information Learned

The best way to memorize the new information is to review it at progressively advancing intervals, for example, one hour, a day, a month and a year. While reviewing the information, you should also include learning to create another copy of the mind map from your mind to ensure you have all the information in your long-term memory. Be sure to use the same colors and topic shapes you used in the original, as this will trigger your mind to recall the association of ideas and words. The best thing about mind mapping is that it makes note-taking feel complete and compact. A whole book summary, lecture, or class can be identified at a glance. It is a brilliantly effective way to comprehend and understand information, study, as well as to review learned information.

How to Create a Mind Map When Taking Notes

Prepare a rough draft: Put together a rough draft quickly. Use printed words, images, and colors to redraft.

Create a topic: Find the focus you will be relying on when thinking. Use as few words as possible. Keeping your focal topics simple will help you connect aspects and ideas precisely and in a comprehensible way. On the other hand, a broader subject will make it more tiresome to work within the future.

Position the topic at the center of the page: The idea is to have a visual representation or pictogram of the central topic. Reserve the use of bold letters in topics for things with no plausible visual form.

Size: Your mind map should not exceed an A4 paper. In order to cover more topics, create a mastermind map that will act as a page of contents for different smaller mind maps. Add more paper when needed.

Use free association to begin the flow of ideas. Write what comes in your mind. Attach branches from the main subject as you generate your thoughts. Minimize your words as much as possible, recording the essentials of all your thoughts succinctly. You can pare the number of words for all the branches as you continue to populate your mind map. Print clearly.

Choose your words briefly: Record simple phrases or single words.

Continue branching: Branch out of your main topic as you continue studying. Try to expound on your thoughts through different ideas. You can draw lines between your thoughts to encourage lateral thinking.

Draw more branches as you develop new ideas from your topic. Spread out as necessary.

Continue spreading out until you fill the map with all your ideas.

When you are done mapping, study the connections carefully and try to refresh their relationships. Have you uncovered any larger patterns?

# Chapter 4: Elements of a Mind Map

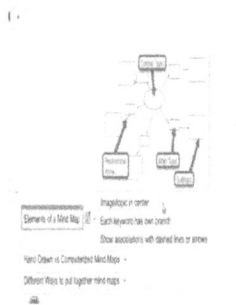

This part will clarify the various components of a brain map just as various procedures and methods of assembling one. This will draw out the absolute most fundamental thoughts encompassing the reasons for mind maps and ideally give you some thought on the best way to make your own brain maps later on. The qualifications between mind guides and psyche planning will be clarified too.

The components of a psyche map are very basic. There is consistently a center focal hub which delineates and picture, a theme, or a focal thought. Here it will be alluded to as the 'Focal Topic'. Originating from the focal subject are typically different branches which lead to different hubs or points. These branches are typically spoken to with 'relationship bolts' prompting different themes. To make things easy to clarify, the principal level of hubs falling off of the focal subject will be alluded in this as 'primary themes' and every one of the accompanying gatherings of hubs will be alluded to as 'subtopics'. Every one of these branches can lead into numerous principle subjects and subtopics. Moreover, there will never be more than one focal subject, as this would require the production of another psyche map.

There are connections between the focal subject and every one of the primary themes, much the same as there are connections between every one of the fundamental points and the accompanying subtopics. The entirety of the principle points, basically, ought to characterize the fundamental subject. As such, in the event that you included them together, every one of the primary subjects ought to portray the focal point in full. At any rate, the primary points ought to be assembled so that you would have the option to determine what the focal subject is simply by perusing the principle themes. The equivalent can be said about subtopics comparable to principle themes.

Things that are firmly related ought to be bunched together under a principle subject. Along these lines, you may have different subtopics that make up a fundamental theme. An undeniable world model will be utilized to exhibit this:

Walt Disney utilized an assortment of brain guides to convey his plans to other people. Thus, state for instance that he was attempting to impart his vision for Disney. In this manner, 'Disney' would be the focal subject, and the fundamental points fanning out from that point would be 'Disneyland', 'Disney TV', and 'Marketing'. Extended from the 'Disneyland' principle subject would be a group of subtopics which would incorporate 'Boondocks Land', 'Experience Land', and 'Tomorrow Land'.

It is evident how this would function extraordinary for arranging purposes. This is the means by which Walt had the option to manage everything from books, comic books, and different distributions, to the remainder of his product, to the amusement parks, to the authorizing, to the music, to the films, and so on. By utilizing mind maps he had the option to regulate an exceptionally perplexing framework in an a lot less difficult way, which permitted his business to get one of the best on the planet.

Hand-Drawn vs. Computerized Mind Maps

You don't have to utilize a refined PC program to make a psyche map. You can coax one out rapidly on a standard piece of paper. Clearly, it is a lot snappier, simpler, and less expensive to make your psyche maps as such. Then again, there has been a blast in the quantity of modernized brain planning devices accessible on the grounds that they have been discovered to be so helpful.

Modernized brain maps offer greater adaptability since you can relocate various subjects and subtopics and rearrange them as much as you wish. They are likewise simple to shading code. This permits you to make more than one connection between the themes and subtopics; this causes you to disentangle complex frameworks in an unmistakable, effectively conspicuous way.

Drawing isn't a prerequisite of either type, however mind map programs make it simpler to utilize pictures to represent various themes or focuses in the brain map. Truth be told, there is regularly a plenty of pictures, representations, and illustrations that you can use. There are additionally unique flowchart-type pictures that you can use in communicating the connections between the points unmistakably.

In the event that you need a stream outline to haul around, you can print these out. Hence, you have both the choice of having an advanced duplicate accessible or you can have a physical duplicate that you can store or keep available to utilize. That implies that in the event that you are on the hurried to some place and won't approach your PC, you can print your brain outlines and use them while you are no more. Then again, you have an advanced duplicate that you can email to yourself and afterward you can get to it from any PC anyplace.

In all likelihood, on the off chance that you begin to utilize mind maps, you will start drawing them out on paper as you experience your day. Be that as it may, as you start utilizing mind planning programming, you will presumably float towards your PC increasingly more since you can make a lot of more clear and inventive structures mind maps inside this product. Obviously, this all should do with how you are utilizing your psyche guides regardless just as what they are being made for.

Different Ways to Put Together Mind Maps

One explanation mind maps are so incredible to utilize is that they are very adaptable and you can utilize them in an extraordinary number of various ways. There are heaps of various ways that you can assemble a brain map. To kick you off, there are three essential methodologies that you can start utilizing right away:

**Open and Get Cracking** — All you do to begin with this technique is put your focal point on the paper, draw a couple of lines going out to primary themes, and afterward begin allowing your plans to ideas, utilizing any instruments that you have available to you to fabricate onto it. This is an exceptionally fundamental strategy, where you start with a thought and you fire developing from the beginning. This is perhaps the most ideal approaches to utilize a psyche guide to think of thoughts.

**Take Notes and Then Mind Map** — Another methodology is to start taking notes and assembling all the data that you need, and afterward plan a brain map out of the data in the notes, arranging the data as you do as such. Clearly, this technique is somewhat further developed than the past one as you are beginning with a pool of data as opposed to simply making a plunge. This would work best for arranging things out and imparting your thoughts.

**Various Levels of Involvement** — This strategy include the utilization and reuse of data. It is ideal to utilize when there are existing psyche guides or prerequisites for various levels dependent on various requirements. At the point when you utilize this methodology, you may utilize various formats that are accessible, or add to old psyche maps. This will permit you to take the data that is as of now there and alter it and modify it in different manners.

The past methods permit you to gain proficiency with the substance better and rename the data dependent on groundbreaking thoughts and ideas. You may even have at least two brain maps open simultaneously so as to include and join the best data from the two. It is ideal to utilize a mechanized program for this kind of brain planning, however you don't need to.

The Difference between Mind Maps & Mind Mapping

There is a major distinction between mind guides and brain planning that is critical to perceive. Psyche maps are the real yield. They are the final product of the psyche planning measure. Psyche maps are commonly comprised of pieces of substance, for example, pieces of codes, pieces of ideas, or pieces of information. These pieces of substance have been gotten together, composed, and orchestrated into a pecking order inside the brain map. These pieces of substance can be as words, numbers, or pictures.

Frequently, basic shapes or hues will be utilized to outline their relationship.

In addition to the fact that you get a superior thought of what you are attempting to assemble by utilizing a psyche map, however others do as well. With the entirety of your data being separated along these lines, individuals are typically ready to comprehend the whole idea in almost no time or minutes. At the end of the day, this is a hugely successful approach to impart thoughts.

Psyche planning, then again, is an innovative cycle which can assist you with arranging your considerations and plan ahead. This cycle permits you to compose your contemplations or develop them better, since you are breaking your thoughts separated in such an unmistakable way. It additionally makes it more clear the connections between the different components being perceived. The purpose of the psyche planning measure is to arrange data and additionally think of thoughts. You can make a psyche map for your very own utilization, or you can utilize it to impart your thoughts or existing information to others in an exceptionally basic manner.

You can likewise utilize mind guides to team up with one another. For instance, you may begin a modernized brain guide and email it to a colleague so they can add to it and send it back to you. For complex frameworks, this can spare a ton of time and vitality since you don't need to stress over talking about each purpose of what you are really going after together. Indeed, everything can be worked and revamped without anybody saying a word.

The demonstration of brain planning causes you to hold data. As it were, experiencing the cycle of psyche planning will assist you with comprehension and take in the data all the more without any problem. Additionally, on the grounds that the data is assembled outwardly, and in small amounts, it is anything but difficult to take it in. At last, the lumping of the pieces of data makes it simple to recollect, since piecing is a mental aide.

Brain planning is one of the best approaches to make and develop your thoughts. As such, the psyche planning measure encourages groundbreaking plans to show. The cycle additionally encourages you to work through your considerations and feelings, making them substantial and useable. Putting a 'pen to paper' along these lines not just makes a difference you to hold the data in your memory, however records it too.

To reiterate, a mind map is the final output of this process and mind mapping is the actual act of creating and organizing ideas and data. So, one is the result and one is the activity that yields the result. This is an important distinction to understand before moving forward. They both have their purposes, and they both allow you to learn and create in unique ways. The following chapters will show you how this is done.

## Chapter 5: Benefits of Mind Mapping

Using Mind Mapping techniques can help put your life in order. You might think that this is an exaggeration. But the truth is, we can all use a little bit of order in our lives right now. We are all living in a wild and crazy world. We are always running around with multiple tasks to do and tons of deadlines to meet. We are always inundated with problems that needed solving. Our minds are working non-stop to come up with ways to help us get through the busy day. We are always thinking of ways to resolve the various problems that are thrown upon us.

Having a Mind Map can help improve the quality of our lives. Below are some of the known benefits of using Mind Maps:

Organize your day, Organize your life

There is an old cliché that tells us that "time is gold." And though it is a saying that has been overused by so many people, the phrase itself still holds true to its meaning. Time is priceless. Once gone, you can never get it back. You'll be left with nothing but regrets. Finding a way to manage your time efficiently can greatly improve the quality of your life.

Mapping out your daily activities can help you become more effective in achieving your goals. You can incorporate in this map all the important things that you do daily in a sequential way. Once you a have a diagram all laid out, you will be able to manage your tasks better. If you are able to allot a reasonable amount of time on each activity, you will find yourself enjoying your life more.

You no longer have to rush from one task to another because you know that you have already allocated a specific amount of time for that specific activity sometime in the day. There is no need to hurry. You can savor the moment and actually be in that moment. You are able to focus all your energy and attention that task alone. When you are focused on your tasks, you are able to produce excellent results. Excellence will only propel you to success.

Cultivate creative thinking

Creating a Mind Map can help boost your creative thinking. Mind Maps usually make use of visual representations of your thoughts and ideas. Because of this, you are forced, in a good way, to come up with various ways to express your thoughts. You can play with words. You can make catchy taglines and memorable quotes. You can play with colors to represent each thought or idea. You can experiment with imagery and pictures to make your Mind Map as interesting as possible.

Mind Mapping can also nurture your creativity is allowing you to explore the vastness of your mind. As ideas begin to branch out form your central concept, there will be times when you will come upon obstacles. When this happens, you will be forced to think out of the box to generate new ideas that can help you overcome those hindrances. This will oftentimes require you to tap into your creative side.

Plan quickly

For you to be able to enrich your life, you need to fill it with as many life events as possible. Weddings, birthdays, engagements and holidays. These are just some of the many events that make life memorable. Take part in these events and make sure that they go smoothly and without a glitch by employing the use of Mind Maps.

Let's take for example a wedding. Planning a wedding is a daunting task to take on. There are too many details to worry about. If you are not careful, you will be overwhelmed by the massive amount of information you will get from friends, wedding websites and magazines, wedding planners and maybe even your future in-laws! Sifting through these can consume a lot of your time.

Laying them all out on a Mind Map can help you streamline the all the data that you've acquired. It will help you eliminate the unnecessary stuff. It will allow you to focus on the things that are important to you. Once you are able to map them out, it will be easier for you to execute your plan. Since you are only focused on the things that matter, you will be able to seamlessly and efficiently carry out your plans. You will be able to make your dream wedding come true.

Take better notes.

At one point or another, you will find yourself needing to take notes. Whether you are in a class, in workshop or in a seminar, taking down notes is an essential part of these activities. Notes will allow you to remember what you've been taught and what you learned. Many people however do not always consider writing a pleasant task. A lot find it boring and exhausting. Oftentimes, you'll find yourself going through pages upon pages of notes that you can barely decipher.

Using Mind Maps to record discussions and lectures will not show you the information you need; it will also show you how these information relate to one another. You will be able to have a better understanding of the subject at hand. You will be able to visualize the topic. Having a mental image of the lessons and lectures will help you remember them easily. This will come in handy during exams.

Know Yourself

When you know who you are, it will be easier for you improve yourself. When you are aware of your strengths and weaknesses, you are able to accept yourself for what you are. Once you are able acknowledge these, you will be able to work through your areas of opportunities and bring out the best version of yourself.

Believe it or not my friend, you can use a Mind Map to be able to know yourself better. You can use the tree-like diagram to lay out the different sides of you. You can map out your strengths, weaknesses, skills, values and beliefs. You can use the diagram as a form of self-analysis. Seeing all of it on paper will give you a better understanding of you.

# Chapter 6: Benefits Of Mind Mapping

Mind mapping boosts your memory

The process of mind mapping involves a unique combination of visual spatial arrangement, color, and imagery that is proven to substantially enhance recall, as compared to conventional methods of learning by rote and note taking.

Mind mapping fosters creativity

Mind maps really go a long way towards encouraging creativity, as well as allowing you to come up with new ideas while brainstorming. The spatial layout enables you to get a better overview, and makes it easy to see new connections in order to create countless thoughts, associations, links, and ideas on any topic.

Mind mapping enhances learning

Studies have proven that mind mapping technique is a very powerful tool for learning. It enhances visual appeal through the use of images, symbols and color, and helps students make sense out of ideas by generating them in meaningful ways. For this reason, this technique is perfect for encouraging active learning, improving confidence, fostering motivation, and for promoting a wide range of levels of ability and learning styles.

Mind mapping supports effective teaching

Mind mapping is a pedagogical tool, whose visibility provides an effective approach for encouraging better understanding in students. It is also flexible, meaning that it can deliver many uses in the classroom.

Mind mapping enhances presentation skills

A study researching about the applications of mind mapping showed that a number of students made clear and compelling presentations with the help of only a trace of their mind map, without shuffling around with notes. The students found it easier to handle challenging questions. This ability of the students to present material in such an effective way was traced back to better recall of the information, since it had been retained and stored in a complex, radiating way, as opposed to linearly. Students were able to internalize the information better because it was their individualized representation of the information.

Mind mapping encourages group collaboration

Mind mapping is a great way to collaborate with others while implementing key projects or developing plans. It enables you to utilize all the members' input in a creative and dynamic way. You can record all the statements or ideas in an appropriate place on your Mind Map, and then discuss openly at the appropriate time.

Mind mapping improves writing skills

A mind map is a great tool for enhancing any form of writing. It helps you get all your key facts and ideas down and organize them in meaningful ways at the same time. Writing then becomes a simple matter of reading the mind map, and then writing a paragraph or sentence on every key word.

Mind mapping promotes critical thinking & problem solving

A mind map can enable you to think more clearly in order to explore the relationships between elements and ideas of an argument, as well as to come up with solutions to problems. It gives you a new view of things, by helping you to identify all the significant issues, and then assess choices in relation to the big picture. It also makes it easier to organize information logically, and to incorporate new knowledge since you are not stuck to a rigid structure.

Uses Of Mind Mapping

Before you start learning the techniques used in mind mapping and how to apply it in your everyday life, it is important you understand its uses. Most writers especially use this tool when they encounter writer's block, or when they experience trouble organizing their thoughts and ideas together. Here are some of the applications of mind mapping:

*Taking meeting notes

Taking notes using a mind map is a great way to capture the ideas discussed in a meeting. This is especially because meetings are usually non-linear and rarely do they follow a specific agenda. In most cases, they are normally filled with exchange of information, ideas, and discussion of countless thoughts, all of which need to be captured. Text notes are technically linear, and this makes it hard to capture ideas discussed in meetings effectively, especially when the meeting is non-linear.

*Book summaries

Mind maps are especially effective when making book summaries. Books, especially non-fiction ones, contain ideas and concepts that you need to capture when reading. If you love reading and you normally take notes on the way, you may have experienced the urge to add an extra concept to a particular idea on another piece of paper. Perhaps you wanted to refer to older notes to make a connection. This may be especially tricky if you are using text, and the ideas may lead to much disorganized notes. Mind maps are great for summarizing information, like that found in books. You can flesh out ideas and concepts using branches to represent your main concepts with your notes and organize them for easier comprehension.

*Project management

While there are several software applications and tools for the purpose of managing projects, you can use mind maps to manage and administer smaller projects. You can start by having your core idea represented as the main project, and then have the following branches set up:

Budget

People

Deadline

Resources

Scope

These branches are the essentials of any project. As such, you can easily use a mind map with them to administer a project. After you set up these branches, you can then review them on a regular basis as you carry on with the project.

*Studying

Mind maps can come in handy especially when you are studying. You can use them in two great ways: one, to make notes during lectures and while studying; and two, to connect the dots when preparing for exams and tests. When you already have a mind map of what you want to recall, you can easily connect the dots using the mind map to comprehend the material at a fundamental level. As such, you will find that you do not need to get the minor details in order to understand the concept. As long as you understand the big concepts and strokes, you can easily implement them (of course, with practice) and solve problems like a breeze.

* Goal setting

Everyone sets goals at one point of their lives. As with most people, you probably rely on pen and paper to write down your goals. This is not a bad idea. In fact, this technique has been around for centuries, and has worked well for many people. However, there is a more effective way of setting your goals: through mind maps. A great reason to use mind maps to set goals is that they are memorable. Why? Because they use visualization, using images and diagrams. As you represent your goals on a page, you can see the outcomes in your mind. Visualizing your goals when setting them is very crucial for their implementation and that is why mind maps are much more effective than note taking on paper.

\*Problem solving

Various approaches are available for problem solving, but a great method to use is the 5W + 1H outline where you ask yourself several questions that need to be answered, in particular:

Who

Where

How

What

When

This is a great application of mind maps, because as you branch out on each section, chances are high that you will find relationships between your answers. These can be easily pinpointed on a mind map. As you find answers to all these questions, you will find that the problem is getting clearer, which will enable the solution become more apparent. To use mind mapping to solve a problem, let your problem be your main idea, and the questions to be represented by branches. Try as much as possible to answer these questions individually, and as you find answers to each one of them, you will most likely come to a solution.

*Brainstorming

The thing with brainstorming is that it usually involves exchange of numerous ideas, and sometimes most of them may not make sense. As such, you can easily capture all the ideas on a mind map, and then reorganize them later to come up with sensible concepts. We are going to expound on this later on.

*Knowledge management

Most people rely on taking notes on paper while reading in order to understand a particular topic. This can be very inefficient at times, especially when you want to recall something amidst all the paragraphs of text. It would be unfortunate and cumbersome to re-read through all these notes while you can easily use a mind map to locate specific ideas on the relevant topic. Rather than using notes to capture information, use mind maps to add knowledge to your bank. Knowledge management can be especially easy and effective, particularly now with the availability of software based mind maps. Take the example of creating a knowledge bank on business networking. There are plenty of PDF documents containing tips, text notes on amazing business networking books, and a mind map on business networking through social media. What is the best way to make a knowledge bank using all these scattered information in different formats and in different files? The trick is to have all this information centralized and tie it in one place. You can represent all this information with a single mind map that will function as your knowledge bank. You can even manage this information using branches in mind maps in a structured way and in an easy format that will be simple to review.

*Getting things done

While mind maps may be great when it comes to representing information in an easy format for easy recalling, they are admittedly not as probable when making a to-do list. You are more likely to benefit from pen and paper in that department. However, that does not mean you cannot use mind maps to get things done. Mind maps can be very beneficial, especially when you use a productivity technique like Agile Results or when you represent your GTD horizons, map them on a mind map, and then transfer the tasks to your task manager.

*Decision-making

Whenever you are faced with a circumstance that warrants making a decision, it always helps to have a range of options to choose from. You can benefit with either of two options: pen and paper or mind maps. While all these methods involve mapping out the options on paper, the distinction in mind maps is that you can make the options visual for easy follow up. This can make a world of difference especially when you are weighing different options. It is easy to spot associations between given options primarily because of its visual nature. This is especially the case when you map out the different scenarios, and it becomes easier to connect various options in order to figure out the best option.

We will talk about the specific ways on how to apply mind mapping in the different areas of your life in the subsequent chapters of this book. But before we can get there, let's take a quick look at the different mind mapping techniques that you can use for success in the different areas of your life before we can narrow it down to the specific areas of your life.

# CHAPTER 7: EDUCATIONAL MIND MAPPING

Educators and pupils have been drawing concept maps and mind maps on paper for years. Visual software programs, particularly brain mapping programs, have automated this procedure, which makes it more effective to emphasise concepts as branches or ideas. This allows for the production of bigger mind maps and the capability to re-organize branches by dragging and dropping them around the map.

It's a known actuality that working with brain maps helps students organize their thoughts and understand concepts better. It is sequential, it can be tricky to use, particularly for pupils who struggle with the procedure. Mind mapping is a more straightforward, non-sequential approach to arrange material, which makes the procedure more coherent, specifically for students that might not be process oriented but aesthetically oriented. Mind mapping can also be known as an assistive tool in which for example, pupils with Asperger or dyslexia will profit in the brain mapping approach.

Enhance reading comprehension

Benefit pupil's accomplishment levels

Boost learning and thinking abilities

Boost retention

Support cognitive learning concept

Use mind maps to understand vocabulary

Vocabulary is your origin of knowledge. But, it is not necessarily easy to recall words of your mother tongue and, of course, learn vocabulary of another language. With the support of a thought map, you may produce maps of word classes in various subjects and add new words into corresponding classes at any moment. The luminous structure of a brain map matches how the human mind functions in diverging a notion.

Mind mapping tools are becoming popular because of their broad array of applications. They aren't used in only business or personal matters but in schooling functions too. These instruments utilize various strategies and methods to produce the practice of studying easier for your pupils. Mind mapping offers a logical sequence of instructional subjects so they're deemed important for pupils. Everybody understands the effects of artwork in your thoughts are strong as compared to the usual tools, so visual guides are used in education purposes to make the learning process simpler.

Photographs and maps are utilized in your mind mapping tools because they could play a significant part in educational atmosphere. Mind mapping is valuable for people who wish to learn through pictures, diagrams and maps. Teachers and students can arrange information regarding a specific subject in a helpful fashion and order. In your mind mapping tools, an item is put in the middle of a webpage and all related thoughts and ideas surround it.

Mind mapping methods are helpful in distributing considerable amounts of data in a simple way. Teachers can arrange and communicate their assignments to their pupils in a smooth and faster manner. The action of lesson preparation gets simple with the assistance of this instrument and can be finished every day. On the other hand, students may arrange their necessary information in a succinct way. They could prepare their texts and notes in a much better manner as compared to the standard ways.

Map of a subject or topic can ensure all the facets of this subject. It makes it feasible to digest the principal ideas and relevant issues immediately with the support of these maps. It would be tough to extract useful information from lengthy concepts. Students may arrange the field in logical arrangement that not only enriches the comprehension of the pupils but also makes the procedure for studying efficient and fast. Moreover, you may connect related issues with the principal idea or motif.

In education, you will need to take care of massive amounts of information and data so you actually desire a beneficial instrument. Mind mapping is helpful for whatever task you perform in educational atmosphere. Mind mapping brings radical changes in studying or learning procedures in a university or college. It will become simple to learn and recall information that is logical, organized, and nicely managed through useful brain mapping tools.

The role of attending courses at a college or school is to learn new things. Teachers and educators use different approaches to produce the educational process smoothly and easily. Mind mapping can also be among these tools that have been proven successful so people use it to get maximum gains. You arrange your efforts, ideas and deliver fantastic results in significantly less time. You might even use mind mapping methods to bring superior results in every area including instruction. It is going to give you thoughts of the technical applications of brain mapping in schooling.

7 tactics to use mind map in education

se head maps to understand vocabulary

Make a language mind map to insert pictures, notes and links into a brain map to include in-depth info and strengthen memory. Definitions, sample phrases, comments, video and audio could be inserted as attachments on a language mind map. The next is a brain map of English collocations using "do" throughout the map, so it's simple to view and you don't forget the collocations at the same glance. Detailed info and more examples could be added to the present word map in any respect.

#use mind map to discover

Grammar is the preparation for successful language learning. But, we constantly hear people whining that grammar learning is a pain. The grammar rules like sentence structures, tenses, and part of language make us aggravated. Usually, we read a punctuation book and write grammar notes to learn grammar; however, it is hard to have a clear general understanding in your mind and difficulty preventing confusion.

Mind maps provide a considerably more effective strategy for sorting out rules. The radiate structure is more ideal for outlining and presenting punctuation points at a bird's eye outline than drilling to specifics. It reflects relationships and reveals relations of various grammar points creatively. Additionally, this map arrangement is much simpler for you to preview and browse in relation to a publication. What is more, you may use eye-catching colours, icons and shapes to make it even more appealing than punctuation books to see.

For instance, if you're studying language parts of speech, you write "English parts of speech" because of the fundamental subject. Branch off the subject with various branches, like nouns and verbs, then divide every branch into detailed catalogues. In cases like this, it's very easy for you to receive the principal content with a glimpse at the map.

#use mind maps to generate a teaching plan

Creating a teaching plan is vital to instruction, but it is generally time consuming. For teachers, mapping an instruction program doesn't just save time but also demonstrates a very clear image of this lesson overall. Here is how I make teaching programs with mind map applications:

First of all, write the title or general content of this course as the fundamental subject on the middle of the picture. Subsequently, branch off the central subject with various main elements in preparing a course, such as teaching goals, details, tools, preparation, actions, and evaluation. Teaching goals lay the basis of the structure and procedure within a course. Details are advice about where and when the course is provided, what will be educated and who will attend. Look for the teaching sources and determine what's going to be utilized in which part obviously. Plan course activities with concrete directions, establish evaluation criteria and evaluation methods to ensure what students will do. Do "3 tests" to guarantee the instruction program is sensible - assess the instruction and working out substances, assess teaching equipment, and assess duties.

#use mind map to do class demo

In course, teachers enjoy using presentations to help their assignments, and pupils occasionally conduct demonstration activities to practice their own learning and communicating skills. PowerPoint and keynote are just two of the most well-known class demonstration tools. But among those challenges with the slideshow is it isn't easily understood the way the whole picture is. Everything you see will be individual slides, and you could not figure out their connections.

That is why many individuals turn to mind maps for course demonstration. Head maps reveal everything in one page. It constructs information in a reasonable manner and reveals the net of connections clearly. What is more, mind maps are somewhat more flexible for demonstration. If you merely wish to demonstrate the articles review for your audience, it is possible to collapse all the specifics. If you would like to concentrate on a distinctive branch when speaking about that area, you are able to drill the branch.

One is slide by slide presentation, and another is complete image dynamic demonstration. You may select any way you prefer. You might even incorporate visual components, such as pictures, icons and colours to the subjects, and add links like site addresses and local documents to enhance your demonstration.

#use mind map to take notes in class

Taking notes is a necessity for students. The most frequent method of taking notes is to copy down exactly what the teacher wrote on the blackboard or replicate contents on the publication to laptops. But, almost all the notes are dotted texts at a linear arrangement that's often lengthy and hard to read. In a mind map, these subjects are expressed with key words or brief phrases after a luminous structure, which compels students to extract crucial information from interminable texts.

Regardless whether the mind map has been created on a blank piece of paper or applications canvas, remember to reveal connections, hierarchies and relations between different pieces of data at a glance. Pictures can be added to subjects to assist comprehending corresponding articles better. Detailed advice can be inserted as a notice, but ensure the information is purposeful. Head map notes will help pupils a great deal when preparing for a test. Assessing with moving over a publication, a brain map is simple to read and proceed with. The procedure for taking notes on a brain map is the way pupils understand and digest the material.

#use mind map to boost students' creativity

Mind maps are manufactured at a luminous construction that's precisely how the human mind naturally works. Pupils have a tendency to copy-paste and imitate others since they're limited by textbooks and particular frames. But if a clean piece of paper is provided, they're far more creative and energetic to share their opinions than normal.

For example, in courses that involve creativity, the instructor can make a new mind map that's a blank canvas and put his idea from the fundamental topic to ask pupils for answers to the thought. Since no prerequisites and limitations are laid out, this may greatly excite students' imagination, and their thoughts burst like a volcano. The next is a brain map of a summertime program; a teacher writes about the fundamental idea and pupils give thoughts on anything they think about, assisting creative thinking ability.

# use mind map to make a book overview

The entire course handed in piles of laptops that mostly include excerpts from the novels we read. Afterwards, some pupils were requested to provide an oral statement on the publication, and the majority of the demonstrations were reciting excerpts instead of plots, topics, and remarks. Evidently, this sort of publication summary did not work out.

Inspiring cases of educational mind mapping

In case you're looking for inspiration in the classroom, look at these gorgeous educational thoughts maps.

# the theory of evolution mind map

This is the kind of map that provides a fast summary of a subject. It could be produced by the instructor in advance of this lesson and spread to all pupils. Students may take more detailed notes during class and attach additional files in the map.

# nouns head map

That can be a grammar mind map that provides a fantastic summary of all kinds of nouns from the English language. Students may create maps such as this one to accumulate all kinds of grammar rules and refer back to them during school.

# Albert Einstein mind map

That is a map of Albert Einstein. Whenever pupils learn about a significant individual, an inventor, writer, scientist or historic figure, they could gather all info about them in this mind map.

# Latin questions mind map

Here is another example of a punctuation mind map. With maps similar to this one, memorizing Latin language, phrases and query words is a good deal more enjoyable. They may also be flipped into slideshows and utilized by the instructor to present new material into the course.

# the geologic time scale mind map

This is a really cool example of a mind map that may be utilized in your geography lesson. It visualizes the various eras with graphics and makes them simple to remember.

# German food vocabulary mind map

Are your pupils still using these older, three-columned note novels to write down words of another language? If this is so, it's about time you present mind mapping!

# publication report mind map

Developing a mind map when studying a book doesn't just improve reading comprehension but also helps students prepare for publication reports.

## Chapter 8: Make the right decisions

"It is always good to have a slow activity before making an important decision."
**Paulo Coelho**

To decide is difficult

The ability to decide "quickly and well" is a skill commonly sought in management. This faculty possessed by "born decision-makers" provides a feeling of confidence and confidence.

Of course, certain decisions are easy to make by instinct and do not require any special effort for this (dressing, choosing a film); at most, we hesitate a little before acting.

Other decisions, such as buying a house or changing trades, require us to integrate many parameters and to mobilize several people.

We need a minimum of information which is sometimes lacking. Often, we are drowned in a deluge of data that must be sorted to see clearly.

To complicate the situation, certain decisions are to be taken urgently or under the pressure of conflicting emotions.

How do we decide?

Analyzing all the parameters can be so delicate that it leads to fear of making a decision. We are then frozen and unable to act.

This phenomenon is all the more frequent as the right to error is less and less authorized in companies.

It also happens that we feel well what should be the decision to take and, therefore, the action that results from it. Despite everything, we postpone the decision in the hope that things will resolve themselves or that new light will reveal the solution.

Sometimes the opposite happens: pressed by the need for action or under the influence of an emotion, we make too quickly a decision to leave this uncomfortable state and see things finally move.

Of course, we must leave a reasonable place for our intuition but by remaining vigilant because many decisions have led to mistakes by lack of information or a belief that later proved false.

In all cases, it must be recognized that it is only when confronted with new alternatives, with life choices, that we really become aware of the need to remember the objectives pursued.

We realize that our values and, therefore, our decision criteria are sometimes poorly defined.

What to do? Which method to use? Should we leave room for emotions, use decision matrices, act quickly?

To decide gently

When we have to make a decision, we want to assimilate a large amount of information from the most diverse origins. We want to be sure that we have included all the alternatives that we have covered all the criteria while leaving a reasonable space for intuitions.

The decision must also be accepted and supported by the greatest number. The ideal is to have a "recipe" that you just have to follow step by step to be sure of arriving at the right decision with confidence.

This method must integrate human, emotional, and intuitive factors as well as rational and factual parameters.

Some methods are chosen

Linear methods

These are linear, rational, and dichotomous methods, the different stages of which are clearly defined. They are available in many variations, but their basic principle can be summarized as follows: defining the problem, identifying and weight the criteria, develop the decision-making structure, identify the alternatives, compare the alternatives to the criteria, decide and finally validate the reasoning.

Among these are decision matrices, Kepner-Tregoe, Electre II, the AHP method.

Their main advantage is to guide the user step by step in a rigid and well-defined framework. They have a formal, systematic, and reassuring side, which can sometimes serve as a support for IT development. The major drawback is related to their rigidity: what to do with our sensations and feelings in such a frozen recipe?

Another problem: these methods lack a global vision: by going through the stages one by one, we only understand with difficulty the problem in all its richness and all its complexity.

Lateral approach

This approach is more creative and uses less direct means. It includes:

• The analogy which consists in establishing a relationship of similarity between the problem posed and another problem already solved;

• The metaphor which consists of reinventing the problem by translating it into a known or imaginary model;

• The reasoning by the absurd which authorizes us to leave the framework, to change references.

Advantages of these methods: they put us in different situations from our daily routines and use imagination, associations of ideas...

The major disadvantage lies in their negative perception, and their side sometimes judged as eccentric.

In addition, these methods require a certain mastery to be animated effectively. This leads to resistance to their use in business. The association of ideas is mainly carried out idea by idea without encompassing the total environment.

The future

We are witnessing the emergence of new techniques that use all of our visual, auditory, and kinesthetic channels.

Information mapping and visualization are decision-making tools that generate the virtuous circle: production of choice, widening of the field of reflection,

" Dilation" of thought, stimulation of brain resources, best choice integrating an infinitely greater number of criteria, and global view of the consequences of the choice made.

The mind map is one of them.

The mind map as a helpful tool at the decision stage

The method chosen is very simple: it consists of browsing, using a heuristic map, a traditional traditionally linear decision-making technique. We will gradually build the decision by assembling the different parts of the puzzle one by one.

To ask the problem

First, let's start by developing a global photo.

Its goal: to provoke an initial confrontation with the problem, to grasp its complexity, and to collect all the data useful for decision-making.

As an exercise and to better illustrate our remarks, imagine that we are going to equip our family with a new car and that the decision will be made collectively.

At this stage, the objective is known, but it is not yet fully defined. It is crystallized by the pictogram present at the heart of the map, here a car.

This pictogram symbolizes, for each participant, a mental and personal representation of all the data and feelings linked to the decision to be made.

NOTE - It is precisely the ease of management of this ambiguity between personal vision and the vision of the group that gives flexibility in decision-making with a mind map.

Next, let's draw from the heart of the map an "alternative" branch that will receive the different possible choices.

In another branch, we list a series of subjects that come to mind without trying too hard to organize them. This branch constitutes a reservoir of ideas, a space for the raw material which will be structured later.

Note that it is not necessary to be connai- all alternatives from the start: running in freewheeling and dropping our thoughts on the card, new alternatives may emerge induction. This can also occur during the review of the objective pursued.

Define the criteria

Another essential step: the definition of the criteria, which will help us to compare the alternatives. This is where the decision-making process really begins.

By clarifying our essential criteria, by defining our values and by linking them to the objective pursued, we are laying down pillars which will serve to filter out the alternatives.

This stage takes on its full dimension during teamwork: in fact, everyone approaches the decision-making process with their own values and their own challenges. By analyzing them together, we listen to the different parts and formalize a consensus.

The criteria are classified into "imperatives" and "wishes." The wishes are prioritized in order of importance, and the imperatives must be satisfied in order to be selected.

NOTE - The list of criteria is well EVIDEM-ing its usefulness in argumentation and communication of the decision.

Code information

With the help of codes and colors, we identify disagreements, moods, preferences. In this way, the intuitive and emotional dimension is integrated and less disturbs the overall process. The card can be illustrated by different sizes of characters, by signs, symbols, or colors to signify the weight of certain criteria.

One can very well imagine that a participant in the decision-making process has from the start a preference for this or that alternative.

In this example, disagreements are illustrated with lightning bolts, preferences with hearts, and imperatives (criteria that must be met) with exclamation marks.

Finalize the goal

At this stage of the process, it is interesting to try to define more precisely the objective pursued. This step, although fundamental, should be carried out once certain positions have been clearly expressed (especially in teams).

Of course, you have to start the exercise with a more or less clear vision of the objective, but you can gain from trusting yourself and letting yourself go in different directions before demanding a precise definition. We thus avoid the blockages which can occur from the start of the decision process.

This way of doing things has the merit of making the group adhere to the objective and its definition.

Following the definition of the objective, certain criteria are further clarified, alternatives disappear, and ... Eureka! Faced with this questioning and visualizing the whole problem on the map, certain alternatives emerge on their own!

Detail the alternatives

The card fills up, and gradually we integrate a large amount of information, both factual and personal. To gain even more finesse, let's decline the alternatives in terms of advantages and disadvantages.

Let it ripen

At this point, the idea is to let the work sit, put into taking advantage of a time of maturation during which our unconscious will continue to function around the problem.

Our intuition can play an essential role here and help us to assess the different possibilities available to us.

By finding the map, we can discover new perspectives and visualize the whole process to bring out the "holes" or the flaws in our reasoning. We must also cut the alternative branches whose imperative criteria are not respected.

By doing so, we reduce complexity and simplify the decision-making process

Decide

To make the right decision, we have to confront the alternatives to the criteria while keeping the objective in mind. This can be done by a numerical weighting in which each alternative receives a rating according to its performance for this criterion. We add it all up, and the alternative that obtains the highest score wins.

Validate

Last step: validate the reasoning by a change of perspective. For that, we redraw the map by placing the retained solution in the center of the page and examine again our objectives: what do we see? Are we satisfied with the reasoning, the solution, and the consequences?

Here we are with the last card, which summarizes the decision adopted.

Value-added heuristic map

Thanks to the mind map, we combine linear decision making with a global visual approach. It allows us to make creative shortcuts and to jump between the stages of reasoning.

NOTE - It's a bit like in a cafeteria queue: in some of them, we must move sequentially through all the dishes from the cutlery to coffee before checkout. In the most flexible, it is possible to compose your menu in a more creative way by returning to back or passing directly from stand to stand, recomposing a unique path for each user of the restaurant.

The mind map favors the management of emotions because these are no longer banished from the process but are really exploited: we can incorporate emotions or contradictions in the form of colors, images, or pictograms which give meaning to the decision.

It is now accepted that our brain functions in images and concepts rather than in words. Our eye has the ability to encompass many parameters to give us an exploitable meaning. Are we not presenting the weather forecast to the general public in the form of geographic maps with icons and pictograms instead of arid lists of climate data?

The use of the view, the space, and the proximity of the information on the map favor the emergence of the decision. As we have already said, the mind map makes it possible to display a new universe. While an individual, limited by the capacities of their short-term memory, will find it difficult to mobilize all the parameters that can influence their decision, they will be able, thanks to the mind map, to approach their choice with a systemic vision of all elements to take into account.

Finally, the map is a very useful vector of synthesis to generate a coherent vision of complexity and communicate the why of the decision and its process.

# Chapter 9: Secrets on Creating Your Own Mind Maps

Mind maps can often be created on a variety of platforms. Such platforms include a piece of paper, tablet/computer drawing application or in online mind mapping software tools.

Beginners are advised to use a piece of paper together with colored pens since this is the best way they can best expresses their thoughts. In addition, drawing out the branches can help you recall the information in your mind map more efficiently.

Before creating a personal mind map, it is advisable to consider seven important tips. These include the following:

1. Get one blank sheet of paper and turn it sideways. Start from its center. It is important to start your mind map in the center to provide freedom to your brain to

branch out in all directions. This would also allow your brain to express itself naturally and freely.

2. Consider using a picture or an image at the central part of the paper to represent the main idea. Apart from helping you use your imagination, a central image provides focus and concentration. It keeps your mind map more interesting and stimulates your brain better.

3. Consider coloring your mind map as much as you can. Colors have the capability to excite your brain in the same manner images do. They add life and vibrancy to your mind map while providing your brain with extra energy for creative thinking.

4. Connect the central image to your main branches using lines. You should then connect branches in the second and third level to those on the first and second level. This is critical since the brain operates by association or in linkages. The brain likes to connect two, three, or four ideas

together. Connecting the branches will allow you to understand and recall things better.

5. Use curved lines instead of straight ones to connect your branches. This is to stimulate your brain as having straight lines can be dull, boring and redundant.

6. Maintain only one keyword per line. Single keywords provide your mind map more flexibility.

7. Make use of as many relevant images as possible throughout

There are no standard or permanent rules that have to be followed when coming up with a mind map. The contents of a mind map revolve around personal choice. For instance, if you want to use more than one keyword or texts to a branch, you can do so. Create a mind map and put elements that would work best for you.

If you are interested in using mind mapping tools, it is critical to consider whether they have important features.

These include the capability to add notes, attachments, links, filter contents, export programs and use of keyboard shortcuts among others. If you find trouble deciding which one to use among the digital tools, here are highly-suggested mind mapping software programs:

It showcases a variety of tools and applications that are designed to help you and a number of people you work with in a number of tasks. Such tasks include brainstorming, staying organized, task collaboration and staying at per with projects. It is considered to be complete project collaboration as well as a management suite. It is made up of an extremely powerful mind mapping and brainstorming tool. It has a ground up design that guides users in organizing their projects, fleshing out jobs that are to be handled in order to complete a project and assigning different duties to individuals. Mindjet is great for mind mapping especially if you are working with numerous people. In addition, this software integrates web tools and services that are often used in businesses and integrates web tools and services that are often used in businesses and personal ventures such as Microsoft Office, box.net, and many more. Users of Mindjet are usually companies that are willing to pay for the software regardless of its rate, which is $ 15 per month per user for the individual plan. For the enterprise plan, it costs $ 30 per month per user.

It is a free application built in Java. It is also General Public Licensed. Its consistent performance and features are the reason why it is preferred by most mind mapping users. It is also flexible and can operate on almost any platform. Freemind is a powerful mind mapping tools, which offer numerous complex diagrams, branches, icons, and graphics that allow you to distinguish notes and connect them as well. It provides an option of embedding links and multimedia in your mind map for easy and quick reference. It also allows you to export your mind map as a PDF file,

Open Document, PNG, SVG, HTML, or XHTML. If you are looking more for function than looks, then Freemind can work for you.

It is probably the oldest when compared to other application. Regardless of this, it has not yet lost its great capabilities and features. The extreme flexibility developed in XMind makes it work on almost any operating system. Users can organize their thoughts as well as ideas using a number of diagrams, designs and styles. The software also boasts of having simple mind maps as well as fishbone style flowcharts. You can also add icons and images to the elements of your mind maps. Links and multimedia can also be added to specific ideas. Many project managers make use of XMind because of its built-in Gantt view, wherein tasks are managed in a way that your colleagues may easily understand and be familiar with. Most of all, XMind is free. On the other hand, if you can afford to spend for a mind mapping application, you can opt for XMind Pro and XMind Plus, which offer additional presentation features, import/export features, and enterprise level features. XMind Pro costs $ 99 for a one-time fee while its subscription and updates cost $ 79 a year. XMind Plus, on the other hand, costs $ 79 for a one-time fee.

It is regarded as the most elegant as compared to the other applications and software. It runs on both OS X and iOS. The iOS version works explicitly well on touch devices like iPad. The software also allows users to easily drag branches around. Additionally, adding and connecting new nodes and sharing your documents have also been made easier. The Mac app supports sharing mind maps with others as well as exporting as a Freemind project or a PDF file. MindNode allows you to hide branches, which are not related with the items you are currently working on. It also allows you to create links on nodes, embed images and screenshots on nodes, and organize branches automatically when they get too crowded or messy. MindNode costs $ 10 for the iPhone and iPad app while the Mac app is $ 20.

It is can be accessed freely. It is also easy to use. Making use of Coggle begins with signing up for a Google account. You can edit an item by simply double-clicking on it. You can also add branches to your map by clicking the plus signs. Coggle assigns different colors automatically to your map's branches; however, you can also click on a branch to bring up a color wheel with which you can choose the colors to use. You can design your mind map by clicking and holding an item to drag around your canvas. Once you are done with your mind map, you can download it either as PDF or PNG file . You can also share it with others and allow them to edit your map if you prefer.

# Chapter 10: Lateral thinking and linear thinking

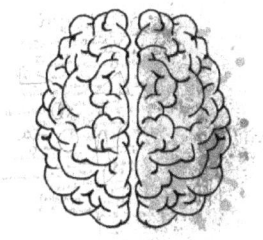

Ideas and concepts of Mind Mapping are connected as the brain does with its neural networks, where both hemispheres work together for better understanding and learning.

This more effective learning combines the qualities of both hemispheres, where the left hemisphere is rational, the analytical one, where logic is located and in the right hemisphere there is creativity, intuition, artistic and musical skills (among many others).

There are moments and problems that, in order to solve them, need logical reasoning and linear thinking, where the left hemisphere responds to those needs. Other problems require imagination, creativity, lateral thinking, which reside in the right hemisphere. Mind Maps stimulate this right hemisphere.

A Mind Map develops that creative part of the brain, lateral thinking, because the human brain associates ideas in a non-linear way, but using creativity, intuition and the representation of symbols, ideas or concepts, being the Mind Map the closest to the functioning of the brain. Mind Mapping encourages creativity, analysis, and connection of ideas or concepts.

Mind Maps and Concept Maps

Both tools have in common that they serve to learn ideas and concepts in a schematic and graphical way, being visually very similar. From there, everything is different. Concept maps require linear, logical, rigidly structured thinking, where concepts follow a sequential process and whose objective is to simplify information with keywords, however, Mind Maps require lateral thinking, imagination, creativity to unite ideas or thoughts represented by words, images and icons linked together by colours, where it is sought to visually outline a concept and do not need a linear development.

Mind Mapping example (Global Warming):

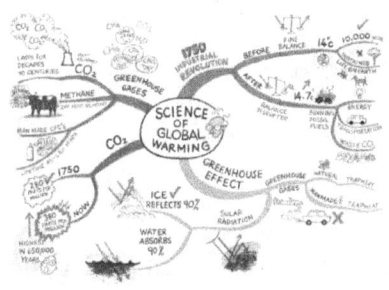

Concept Mapping Example (Climate Change):

WHAT ARE MIND MAPS FOR?

"As you navigate through the rest of your life, be open to collaboration. Other people and other people's ideas are often better than your own. Find a group of people who challenge and inspire you, spend a lot of time with them, and it will change your life." – **Amy Poehler**

Benefits of mind maps

We are going to list the benefits of Mind Mapping.

• Mind Maps are an excellent learning tool and make it easy to remember information by organizing it visually. By adding images and drawings to the text, the brain is easier to learn and assimilate than if there is only text, to which it really does not pay much attention, nor does it allow to remember properly, as has already been said before.

• Helps to memorize information due to the associations that are created between images and concepts, favouring the learning of long or complex subjects to understand. Allowing the study more efficiently and in less time.

• Also in the educational field, it facilitates the beginning of study and breaks down barriers such as laziness, procrastination and rejection of said study.

• Activate the right hemisphere promoting the development of creativity and imagination.

• They allow the collaboration and participation of all the members of a work group in the business and educational world, where everyone feels valued and active listening and participation are developed.

• They allow, through online tools, group mind maps to be created without the members of the work team being together, each one being able to do it from home, favouring the flow of ideas at the same time for all members regardless of where they are and of the computing device they use.

• They have a mnemonic function when remembering images, a large amount of information associated with said image, where the saying "a picture is worth a thousand words" is the best example to illustrate it.

• It simplifies the process when it comes to capturing all the information by reducing pieces of information or concepts with a single word or image, favouring the generation of ideas, solutions and improving decision-making.

• They facilitate the capacity for synthesis, organization and analysis of study topics, improving productivity and efficiency. They are clear, specific and precise.

• The use of colours reinforces the connection between associated concepts or ideas and if they are different and striking, even more. The brain works internally with associations so they help to retain information more effectively.

• It allows to structure presentations, exhibitions of educational works or business projects that provide a general idea at a glance. Helps to slice and dice an overall project into sub-projects in a more manageable way.

• It allows to visualize the weaknesses and strong points of a project or presentation and to work on them, organizing ideas in a clear and precise way.

• It is very versatile and adaptable to any situation and use.

# Chapter 11: Know What Type Of Writing You Are Going To Do and Who You Are Writing For

In this chapter, we will be focusing on basics in writing that will help you define your purpose and when you finally found it, it will serve as your guide from where your key points will be. In the case of idea mapping, the ideas that will pop out of your mind will be varied and sometimes, random. When you have established the type of writing and your purpose for writing, you will be able to narrow down your thoughts and ultimately, be able to come up with a good idea map that will give you better results in what you will be writing about. Here are basic types of writing:

**Expository writing.** This type of writing aims to discuss about a certain topic mainly to just inform the reader and expound about it. This writing mainly focuses on facts and gives the reader the part of expressing his or her opinion about the certain subject. An example of this is your textbooks in school. Those thick textbooks for your chemistry subject that you are using in order to pass your exams. It could also be an article explaining about how you can create a certain dish starting from its ingredients and procedure itself mainly focusing on facts and just giving you the information you need.

**Persuasive writing**. This type of writing has a purpose of convincing and persuading the reader about what an author has to say. It can be a combination of stating facts and expressing opinions about a certain topic in order to influence the audience. Opposite to expository writing, persuasive writing heavily emphasizes on opinion in order to convince hence, its name, persuasive writing. An example of this is an article of advertisement for a particular product, let's say a new burger in a fast-food restaurant. It could be written as review of how good it tasted and how the writer or the one who evaluated it found it worthy of the price. It can also be your favorite car magazine where they put opinions on the newest model of cars aside from giving out the technical specifications.

**Narrative writing.** This type of writing aims to tell or report a story that may be a fact or something made-up or what you call a fiction. An example of this is a biography or maybe even an autobiography of a famous person. It could be an article of the success story of a prominent person in a big industry let's say, the world of real estate. It could also be your favorite novel you are reading during your free time. In this type of writing, the author may tell the story in the character's point of view and putting the author's feet in the character's shoe and also making the readers feel like they are the ones going through the experiences of the character in the story.

**Descriptive writing**. This type of writing aims to stimulate the reader's senses by enumerating specific details of things they tell like describing an image of a person by how his or her face looks beautiful in a detailed way, let's say thick eyebrows and dark brown eyes. The writer can also stimulate the reader's senses by telling how the image they are trying to describe smells like, how it tastes like, and feels like. Because of this, descriptive writing gets the "most detailed award" among the four types of writing.

Now that you have identified different types of writing and their purpose, think at what you are going to write about, is it an essay? Are you writing a novel? Define your purpose for writing and from there, create your idea map. Aside from knowing what type or types of writing you are going to use, it is also important to know who you are writing for. Your readers will also have to be considered when writing. Are you writing an article about a product?

Make sure it is persuasive enough for consumers to really patronize it.

Are you a medical expert writing for lay people? Make sure you modify your terminologies and use simpler words for your readers to comprehend what you are saying. If you can't avoid a certain terminology, define it and expound about it so that your audience will be able to understand it. Are you planning to create a book for children? Make sure your words are very simple and make your writing fit for them. Whatever that is you are writing, make sure you will adjust to your readers and in that way, you will achieve success in sharing your ideas in your writing.

# CHAPTER 12: IMPROVE YOUR MEMORY WITH MIND MAPPING

Memory can lead to the accomplishments of many astonishing feats. Take for example the story of Mozart visiting Rome in 1770, when he was 14, and listened to Allegri's Miserere in the Sistine Chapel. The half-hour long piece of music was considered so special that the Vatican forbade its publication, but after the concert Mozart wrote down the entire piece of music from memory. Or more recently, Memory champions have been setting world records which seem nothing short of miraculous to ordinary people. It is often assumed that such people must have extraordinary brains or be amazingly clever. However, in 2002 scientists put this assumption to the test and performed a range of tests on highly ranked memorizers at the world memory championships held annually. The tests revealed that the memory champions' brains showed no differences to that of ordinary persons. However, it was discovered that nine out of the ten memory champions were simply using a technique called 'the method of Loci', which dated back to ancient Greece. This method is based on Location and imagination. It was therefore concluded that a good memory is simply a skill, and a skill that can be learned - at any age.

The main principle of memory techniques is linking the thing to be remembered to some other idea - this is known as association. When your memory has meaning, your brain gives it a tag that makes it much easier to retrieve. A similar process is achieved when you see something in context or linked to some other idea which provides a tag for the idea. If you imagine your memory as a library, it is clearly much easier to find a particular memory if it has a tag attached to it. You will be amazed how dramatically you can improve your ability to remember things if you use combinations of association, vibrancy and imagination.

The best technique that encourages you to use association and imagination is Mind Mapping. Mind Mapping was invented by Tony Buzan in the 1960s, although the learning principles of Mind Mapping have been around for hundreds of years and have been used by some of the world's greatest thinkers. Tony Buzan states that it is the ultimate thinking tool - a creative and effective means of thinking that literally 'maps out' your brain. Mind Maps are an ideal tool to use as a memory improvement tool, not only is it extremely simple but it can have an immediate impact on memory, creativity and your ability to concentrate. Mind Maps have a natural structure that radiates from the centre and uses lines, symbols, words, and images according to a set of natural and brain-friendly rules. A long list of boring information can be turned into colourful, memorable, highly organised diagrams that reflect the brains natural way of thinking and encourages synergetic thinking.

Imagination and association are the two main principles that make Mind Mapping so effective. By developing creative skills you are not only improving your ability to come up with innovative ideas you are also, by default, enhancing your ability to remember things. This is because creativity and memory are vertically identical mental processes - they both work best when you are using imagination and association.

# Chapter 13: Examples of Mind Mapping and Mind Mapping Software

Examples and explanations of the multiple approaches different kinds of people may have.

Now that we have looked at how to make a mind map, let's take the time to study a few other examples in depth. First, let's look at some examples of other people's mind maps. Most people doing mind maps for business, education, or non-profits are using some form of mind mapping software. We will credit that software in these examples and provide their URLs in the appendix.

Examples of Mind Mapping

Business Examples:

This particular mind map is a company's revenue forecast from a variety of locations around the world. Obviously, this would be a large multi-national corporation and this mind map would be developed by the Accounting/Financials Department. Let's look at how they structured this mind map.

The first thing you will notice is that this mind map is not quite as free flowing as many others we will look at. It is particularly structured (as it comes from a particularly structured profession) and yet it follows the rules of mind mapping.

1. In the center is the core concept or challenge. Here the center id Revenue Forecast contrasting the budget versus the actual and the +/- for the entire company. You will also notice that there is a note and an attachment also in the center. This displays one of the best features of mind mapping, and that is the ability to attach supporting documentation and links to the map.

2. In this mind map, the largest branches

coming off of the center are the areas of the world where this company has offices. These branches are named North America, South America, Asia and Europe. These are the primary locations that will produce revenue for the company. Each of these primary locations shows the budget, actual, and +/-. You will notice there is a note attached to North America, but no documents attached to any of the four branches and only North America has a note.

3. Now each of the branches breaks off into three twigs. These twigs are sub-locations within the larger location, and each provides the budget, actual, and +/-. Again notice that US has a note attached. No other branches have notes.

4. I am sure that there could be even more smaller twigs going off of each of the twigs in #3, that might go to states/provinces or cities etc. If a new location comes on board, it is very easy to add that new information to this mind map and still see it all at a glance.

Now think about the usual, traditional monthly revenue reports we are all used to seeing whether in our businesses or if we belong to a social or nonprofit organization or serve on any type of board. We are used to seeing a truly linear flow of information that would list this same information in either a spreadsheet that had to be read from left to right, or an outline that would be read from top to bottom. Neither of these more traditional ways of organizing this information allows you to see **at a glance** the whole financial picture for your company for that month.

For example, with this mind map you can see that this company had revenue for the month that was 2.8 percent above the projected budget. Good news I am sure, but it hardly tells the whole story. Just where did this additional revenue come from and did every location meet or exceed their budgets? With a traditional spreadsheet, you might have to dig three or four pages into the report to get this information. With this mind map, you can see at a glance that North America and Europe over performed while Asia and South America under performed. Furthermore, you can see that most of your over production came from Germany while the greatest under production was in Peru.

Think how long it would take to dig this information out of a traditional financial report. So even though we said at the beginning that this mind map was fairly structured and not as free flowing as some other might be, it is still remarkably advanced in showing you the whole picture at a glance. You can see immediately why presenting even traditional financial information in this format is so conducive to increased productivity and efficiency.

Now let's go to a different type of example. Let's look at an example that is actually a mind map of how to go about using mind maps. This one is a little more unusual to look at, more creative and colorful, and gets you to the same place in terms of organizing information in a way that makes it easy to see and act on.

http://mappio.com/

We will examine this mind map in the same way we did the previous one. Here you have the central concept or image as Team Mapping Method. This group is going to develop a method for mind mapping as a group or team.

1. Once again in the very center of the page you have the most significant concept/image or in this case goal. In this mind map, as opposed to the last example, you see a lot of creativity, color and fun in placing the central concept on the map.
2. The branches of this mind map are the steps that must be gone through to get to team mapping. These branches include:
·Defining the topic

·Individual idea maps

·First consolidation

·Second consolidation

- **Prioritization**
- Taking Action

Something interesting about this mind map is that the branches are numbered 1-5 and the tasks to be done follow in that chronological order. This is not necessarily true of all mind maps. In fact, it is probably less true than not.

3. There are many twigs off of each one of these branches. These twigs are not necessarily completed in any order except that the entire branch is completed before moving on to the next branch. Branch one is completed before you move to branch two. This is also not the norm for mind maps. However, the twigs within branch five have a "do this OR do that" and at the same time within branch five you also have other twigs going on such as "each person defining his top five priorities."
4. It would be easy to add smaller, more detailed twigs off of the ones already here to change/add or delete information from any step in this mind map.

Again, this mind map allows you to see at a glance, on one piece of paper, the entire Team Mapping Process from identification of ideas to assignment of tasks. Even Gantt charts and other project management tools do not give you this kind of flexibility.

Note: Gantt Charts are project management tools included in every type of project management software. A Gantt chart is a bar chart that was created by Henry Gantt to illustrate the scheduled timeline for a project. A RFP is a Request for Proposal that is also included in all project management software.

Is this beginning to make more sense to you and are the benefits of mind mapping becoming clearer now? It takes walking through several of these, and comparing them with what we are used to seeing, before it becomes clear how to make one and what its advantages might be for you. So again, if you want to get the most out of this eBook be sure you are working along with us on these examples. Let's do another one.

The following mind map will look very different to you as soon as you glance at it. This is just another way of presenting the information so that it is organized, linked and you can tell at a glance what is going on.

1. In this mind map it is Innovation that begins the process; therefore, in the middle of the page you find a circle with the word Innovation and what it applies to in the setting where the mind map is made. They are looking at Innovation as changes in thinking, in things, in processes and in settings.
2. There are a multitude of branches off the keyword innovation—it is just that the maker(s) of this mind map feel very comfortable with circles, so they have made their entire mind map in the form of a circle with many internal circles. There are five green and five blue circle branches growing out from the key word innovation. The green circles are physical tangibles while the blue circles are intangibles. For instance, one of the green

circles is Staff/Patrons while one of the blue circles is Flexibility.
3. In this mind map all of the outer circles are linked to the keyword Innovation, but they are not linked to each other. Notice that none of the outer circles have lines attaching them to each other. You can see from this how there can be a wide variety in how a mind map is made depending upon the circumstances, and what you want to convey. Different people/groups with different needs will want to use the mind map that best suits their needs.

Let's just look at a couple more, and then move on to the various software programs that are available for designing mind maps, if you do not want to do them freehand.

Personal Examples:

The next mind maps we will review will be ones that are used in one's personal life. The first one is a life planner, and the second one is an exercise in discerning your life's purpose. Following our discussion of these two mind maps, I will review several software programs.

In this example, the author is using a mind map to plan aspects of his life. This could be done in any way that the author wants to do so. As you can see in this mind map, there is a calendar linked to the central image of Life Planner. All of the branches coming out from the Planner might or might not have dates attached, but if they do, the dates would also be recorded on this calendar. For instance, one of the twigs coming off the Family branch includes birthdays and these would be recorded in the Planner calendar. This same twig might be connected to the Personal and the friendship branches as well. There might be doctor appointments on twigs from the Health branch and any number of calendar dates might come off the Spiritual, Community, Recreation, or Career Branches. It is easy to see how this mind map might expand and change almost continuously.

This mind map is for discerning on your part what the purpose of your life may be.

1. The central image/concept is Discover Your Life Purpose with many branches and twigs flowing out from the center.
2. This mind map has eleven different branches, but there could be many more, or there could be far fewer. It is up to the individual and the aspects of their life's purpose that they might want to explore.
3. Each of the eleven branches in this mind map has at least one twig for a subtopic but several have as many as three. You could have as many as you have ideas for. In fact, you should keep adding and adding twigs along the appropriate branches until you can think of no more.
4. This Life Purpose mind map could lend itself to smaller more detailed twigs coming off the first set of twigs, and keep drilling down until all ideas and concepts have been detailed.

Now you have seen a wide variety of types of mind maps, some very simple and some fairly complex. There have been examples of mind maps for holding meetings, for developing projects, for evaluating financial information, business innovation, personal life planning and personal life purpose discovery.

Mind Mapping Software

There is a multitude of software programs available for those who would rather use a program than draw it out themselves. Do not think that just because you use a software mind mapping program that your map will be dull, lifeless and colorless. That is just not true. There is such a variety of programs on the market, and they all have a variety of features. Some will be very uncomplicated and some complex. Some will be very workman-like while others will be playful and fun oriented. Some of this software is free and can be downloaded while other programs are proprietary and must be purchased. Let's take a look at some of both types:

The best mind mapping software will tell you at a glance what the map is about, what the important branches are, and how they are connected and linked. A good mind map will tell you a lot about its substance just by its shape. The best mind maps will require you to use both the left and right side of your brain to process the information it displays, and be able to act on it. No conventional way of organizing information and presenting it can do that.

Which of these software programs are the best? That depends on personal preference, but there are some programs that stand out. First, let's look at the software that was used in the previously discussed mind maps.

Best Proprietary Mind Map Software

The first two mind maps in this book—The Agenda and The Revenue Forecast—were developed with MindView software.

MindView 4

This is one of the best business mind mapping software programs on the market today. Why? Because Mindview4 collaborates extensively and easily with mind maps of all kinds. There is a terrific online workspace where you can share an online map as well as the many tools that project managers need to get their job done. MindView4 integrates well with MS Office, so you have all the on the job tools you need to be productive, to brainstorm with your team and to organize your information in a better, more accessible manner, so that you can act on it faster. MindView's integration with MS Office includes not only Project and Excel, which you would expect, but also Word, Powerpoint and Outlook.

Other features of MindView4 that make it a leader in the business community. This includes Gantt Charts, Timelines, Work Breakdown Structures, and Team Assignments. There are RFP's, marketing plans, strategic plans, Outline reports and Knowledge. You can attach an Excel file to your MindView4 mind map or you can transfer your mind map data to Excel or Project. MindView4 lets you work with your remote team members by sending your mind map by email and offering a free online software package to open it, and use the Shared Workspace that we mentioned earlier.

The next example of a mind map was designed by Philippe Boukobza, as explained in Jamie Nast's book Idea Mapping (2009, John Wiley & Sons).

The next mind map (Innovation) was designed without any software but the following two (Life Planner and Life Purpose) both used eDrawsoft.

eDrawsoft

This software was developed in 2004 with the goal of developing drawing software that is easy to use and of high quality, but that does not cost a fortune. They succeeded. This is easy to use, is a web based software with Active X controls. Everyone can pick this up and begin drawing very easily

Here are some other important software programs that we have not yet delved into in depth.

Mind Map/New Concept Draw

This is one of the easiest mind mapping software programs on the market. It is so flexible and creative that it will make designing your map and integrating it with other applications very straightforward. You can write in a wide variety of languages as well. You can create dashboards for your team members, use the GTD feature (Getting Things Done), and use the features for acting on and tracking results of what is in your mind map.

You can store an unlimited amount of links and associations, use color, creativity, imagery, and space to design a mind map that will be immediately understandable and easy to remember. Every Mind Map is unique and has its own way of embedding itself into the mind and memory of the users. Version 6 has such an abundance of new and creative functions that it jumps up in the rankings for top of the line business mind mapping software. One of the most important upgrades in 6.0 is that the 3D feature is now fully functional. You can change the background to 3D also to make it more visually appealing as you can see from the example above.

There are excellent new features in MindMap 6 and iMindMap 6 for creating your branches, and connecting them easily by dragging the line to the branch or box, that you want to connect it to. This simplifies the software for the user and leaves a finished mind map that is easy to comprehend for the reader. This is an excellent upgrade to the MindMap software family.

Nova Mind

Nova Mind 5 is the standard bearer for this product and Nova Mind 8 is the newest version designed for Windows 8. Nova Mind 8 is a complete revision of this product and has a "touch first" orientation that allows the user to drag, pinch, or tap the data on the screen. There is new functionality built into this as well. You can add new twigs simply by dragging a line out from an existing branch. The presenter mode is one of the most exciting and versatile features of Nova Mind.

Nova Mind is one of only a handful of mind mapping programs, which allow you to lay out your branches wherever you want or need them in a free layout program. It is user friendly, versatile and intuitive. Nova Mind has multiple languages, and it caters to project managers and screenwriters with specific modules for them. Export and import Office files easily with Nova Mind. It is a magnificent product for both individuals and businesses.

SpiderScribe

This is a great mind mapping software program for beginners as it is a pure drag and drop format. If you have never made a mind map, you will love the help page and the video that describes how to use the software and how to incorporate what you need into your map. You can add maps, text, events and images, with simple drag and drop functions. It is just as easy then to make connections and links or move data and images around wherever you want them.

Incorporate text, images, maps and events, by simply dragging and dropping "stencils" into the workspace, arranging and connecting them—all in an easy-to-understand user interface. Even if you have never created a mind map before, you will find the process to be easy and intuitive. Unlike some programs, the developers of SpiderScribe provide a help page and demo video that are clear and easy to follow.

# Chapter 14: Potential Uses of Mind Map

In this chapter, I will discuss how you can apply Mind Mapping in your personal and professional life. I tried to be as comprehensive as possible without being too tedious. What I want you to understand after reading this chapter is that Mind Map will improve your efficiency and effectiveness throughout every area of your life. If you are already somewhat familiar to the technique of Mind Mapping, you will find new potential uses in this chapter. Also, for those of you who are using Mind Map in many of these areas and want to take the technique a step further, I have dedicated a chapter (**Chapter 6**) for that. Meanwhile, let's dive right in.

Brainstorming

One of the most popular and most effective uses of Mind Map is brainstorming. Several features of Mind Map make it an ideal tool for brainstorming. First, Mind Map focuses on one central keyword, so it reduces possible digression and directionless thoughts. Second, Mind Map provides a framework for free association: you can write as many stemming words from a keyword and expand to as many degrees of separation you'd like.

Association is the key to finding new ideas. If you look at the examples of historic invention or scientific breakthrough, you will inevitably notice a pattern where the inventor or scientist got the idea while thinking about something that has some kind of association with the idea. Bill Bowerman got the idea for the "waffle-sole" shoes which launched Nike to be the mega-million giant while having a waffle for breakfast. Also, German Chemist August Kekule was able to figure out the elusive nature of the benzene ring after seeing six snakes forming a circle while holding onto one another's tail in a dream.

Third, the act of writing down the central topic and the ideas around it on a paper has a subtle yet powerful effect on your brain. It gets your brain to generate ideas much better and effectively than you would if you would try to do it all inside your head. You will be able to observe this firsthand if you try to brainstorm in your head and on paper. Finally, the usage of keywords and short key phrases speeds up the process, which is crucial to the brainstorming process. As many of the creative geniuses say in common, the more ideas you get, the higher the chance you'll get a great idea. Therefore it is important that you get as many ideas as you can in as short a timespan as you can. Mind Map is an ideal tool for this; it takes care of both the number and the speed with its principle of association and keyword-orientedness, which I explained in Chapter 1.

When brainstorming with Mind Map, there are several considerations in addition to the speed and number of ideas. In order to let your creative juice to flow, you need to tone down your inner critic for awhile. You might make some spelling errors in the process, or wonder if a particular keyword deserves a place in the Mind Map. In the grand scheme of things, these are insignificant issues. Above all, you need to make sure you get as many ideas as possible. Censoring yourself in the process is only counterproductive. You can sort out these minor errors later, or you might not need them at all!

Use multiple colors and apply a varied style if that helps. You might find the colors and curved lines stimulate your brain and give you some great ideas. Often the process of writing down ideas along with a free association process is enough to get your creative engine going. Once you start using Mind Map for brainstorming, you will see how powerful this simple technique can prove to be.

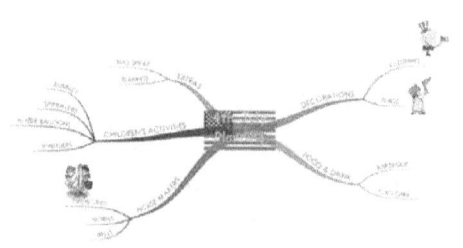

Figure 4-1. Example of Mind Map used for brainstorming on 4${}^{th}$ of July plans.

Group brainstorming

As you read along, you will find that Mind Map can be applied on both personal and interpersonal/organizational levels. While you will be the only one who creates and uses the Mind Map when you use it for personal purposes, more than one people can participate in the process of creating and using the Mind Map when used in a group setting. Brainstorming is an excellent example where this comes into play—an area where you can observe the fascinating interplay of different frameworks of thinking.

Group brainstorming can be much more effective than everyone playing solo. This is where the sum of the parts becomes greater than the parts themselves. When people and ideas interact, they give rise to new and improved ideas which have not been accessible before. And Mind Map plays a vital role in this.

When using Mind Map as a group brainstorming tool, there are several ways to do it. First, people can draw their own Mind Maps and share them with the group after they're done. Second, all members of the group can take turns to participate in creating a group Mind Map. Then there are combinations of these two methods; for example, the group can break into subgroups which will bring their Mind Maps to the whole group. Or, individual members can prepare a Mind Map on a subtopic of a subject and be brought together to complete the group Mind Map one cluster at a time.

This method of group brainstorming has several advantages other than the innate effectiveness of Mind Mapping. First, the members can flesh out their ideas fully by expressing them on a Mind Map. Second, along the same line, the participants won't have to worry too much about their ideas being rejected prematurely, because everyone is asked to complete their own Mind Map first or is given equal opportunities to participate in a group Mind Map. Third, by capturing all the ideas on a single Mind Map, the group can make sure that no idea goes unnoticed or gets lost in the process. And last, if executed properly, the process can result in better ideas because all the members are equal participants and can claim ownership of the ideas as a group product. All in all, Mind Map can dramatically increase the effectiveness and the quality of the end-product (the ideas) of group brainstorming.

Creative writing

By the word "creative", I don't mean it in a narrow sense like poetry or fiction writing, while those are certainly part of it. I want to include all kinds of writing where you are writing something new yourself. That includes essays, proposals, reports, theses, and other technical or practical documents. In fact, all of these can be said to be "creative writing", because you are creating something new from scratch.

For many of us, writing something from scratch can be painful. Unless writing is one of your strong suits, you can feel hopeless when you face a blank sheet of paper or your computer screen with a new document open. Mind Map can remove much of this frustration and get you going in writing mode much faster. When you were in high school or college, how did you approach your writing assignment, essay, or theses? We were told to come up with an outline first; however, there are some shortcomings to outlining.

First, when outlining, many people feel they need to come up with something neat and tidy while we can't have a full grasp of the subject on the first attempt. Therefore we often feel discouraged when certain blind spots or "fuzzy areas" come up while outlining. Second, by trying to think chronologically from the beginning to an end, we put a limit on our creativity. The ideas don't come necessarily in a linear order. Rather almost always the ideas come randomly at first, then you arrange it in an order which makes the most sense. Trying to flesh out an outline first restrains the brainstorming function of your brain because you are going against the natural tendency of the brain.

Now don't get me wrong; I am not trying to say that outlining is useless and you need to throw out outlining altogether. My point is that while an outline is an essential part for a coherent and organized writing product, you can't come up with a good outline by tackling the outline first.

What's the alternative? Well, in order to address the shortcomings addressed earlier, it is clear that you need to have a process of pouring out ideas so that you need something to work with, the "basic ingredients" for outlining. Here is where Mind Map comes in. Mind Mapping can help you not only in brainstorming for the content, but organizing them into a meaningful outline as well. In fact, you can create an outline in the form of a Mind Map, rather than traditional list-form outline. First, you want to write everything you know about or have done research on a subject down on a piece of paper, and Mind Map is a perfect way to do this. Once you can see all the information and bits of ideas on a piece of paper, you can start to organize the ideas in a meaningful way. You can choose what to write on and what to leave out, then move the ideas around until it makes a coherent outline.

So next time you need to write something, use the guidelines I've just presented and see how much more quickly and effectively you brainstorm and more coherent and convincing your outline becomes. In fact, this is how precisely I wrote this book. I've done a full-on brainstorming on the subject of Mind

Map, then organized the topics into a draft Mind Map that looked like this:

Figure 4-2. Mind Map used for planning and outlining this book.

Now I have to confess, I haven't been the best writer in the world when I was in grade school. However, ever since I've used this technique, I've found writing much easier and enjoyable than before. One of the challenges I had in the past was to figure out what I would write on. Now, with the help of Mind Map, I can come up with a full outline in less than thirty minutes!

Organizing information

Earlier in the book I've briefly mentioned that Mind Map can serve both the creative side and the analytical side of your brain. So far we discussed how Mind Map can be used to cater the creative side. Yet, Mind Map can be equally effective in the analytical usage. Let me start with one of the most common examples, which is organizing information.

In the previous paragraphs explaining how you can use Mind Map for creative writing, I have touched on how you can first brainstorm then organize the ideas, all using Mind Map. In fact, Mind Map can be used to organize just about anything. What makes Mind Map great for this purpose is the focus on a central keyword and the clustering which enables you both the snapshot view and detailed information.

You can organize course materials, professional information, systems and processes, to-do lists, or even shopping lists. You can try Mind Mapping wherever you feel overloaded with information or need more clarity. As you get good at it, you will be able to create your own "cheat sheet" of whatever information you need to better understand and handle. Not just take my word for it; I want you to try it for yourself. When you have time, create a Mind Map of what you've learned in your chemistry class, the various elements of your next project, or the options for your next family vacation plan including the different interests of your family members. You will be amazed at how clearer your thinking seems to become, and how the information which seemed so overwhelming feels more manageable.

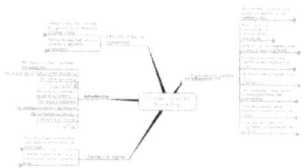

Figure 4-3. A sample Mind Map used for book summary.

Note taking

This use and the next several ones can be classified into the broad category of organizing information. If you are a student, Mind Map can give you an unfair advantage over others because this powerful tool hasn't gone mainstream yet among students. Students often fall prey to one of the two extremes of note taking. They write either too little so they have trouble with recollection, or too much so they don't have any room left to really take in the lecture and process the information. The point of note taking is not to reproduce the entire lecture later. It is supposed to act as a supplement in your studying. Therefore, as a general rule, you need to find a medium ground between the two extremes.

Not all the materials in a lecture are created equal. Some are key points which are crucial for your understanding of the subject matter, while others are "just-so-you-know" information. In order to effectively identify what matters and what doesn't, you need to be able to grasp the big picture at all times during a lecture. Here is where Mind Map comes in. While some people suggest that you only take notes in a Mind Map format, I don't suggest you do so when you are starting out. Identifying what matters is a skill which takes some time to master. Until you become more adept in separating the wheat from the chaff, I suggest you use Mind Map as an accompanying device to your main note-taking method.

Here's how you do it. Get a separate sheet of paper besides your notebook, and write down the name of the class or the subject of that particular lecture in the center. Then, as the lecture proceeds, try to follow along by using keywords and key concepts as the basis of your Mind Map note. Let the details be handled by your textbook or your main notebook. The purpose here is to draw a big picture, and get used to classifying and processing information as they are presented real-time.

As you use this method of note-taking more frequently, you'll notice that your thinking and comprehension improves. You'll be more efficient in your studying, because you will be able to better understand how the key concepts relate to each other. In the end, you will be getting better grades while studying less. It is all about efficiency and effectiveness, not just hard work. And Mind Map is a great tool which enhances both efficiency and effectiveness in anything that has to do with your mind.

Meeting notes

Note taking is not confined in the classroom setting. One of the examples where Mind Map can be useful for note taking outside of academia is meeting notes in a corporate environment. You can use Mind Map in real-time as I have explained earlier, or as an organizing tool after the meeting, depending on the propensity of the user or appropriateness for the occasion. When using Mind Map for this purpose, there are several tips that will increase the effectiveness of the Mind Map. First, try using different shapes or colors for each participant and different symbols for the nature of a comment—a proposition, a question, a request for follow-up, etc. When doing this, try to make a category for items that are actionable or require further action. You can even collect everything of this nature and list them as a subtopic of the Mind Map.

With the advent of computer-based Mind Map software, the possibility for using Mind Map for meeting notes has increased exponentially(In the **next chapter** I will explain more on how computer enhances the functions of Mind Map). You can easily share a Mind Map with all the participants who can make revisions and clarifications on what they have said or meant. Then, the revised Mind Map can act as an action plan which can keep all of the members engaged. The advantage of Mind Map over traditional methods of group communication comes from the increased clarity Mind Map is able to provide; everyone can understand the whole landscape more clearly, and this is more conducive to positive action and problem-solving.

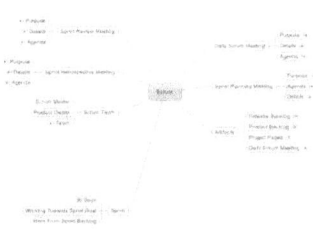

Figure 4-d. Example of a "rough draft" meeting notes

Study/learning

Mind Map is simply a great tool for studying and learning. In fact, author and college professor Toni Krasnic wrote a great book on this subject, **How to Study with Mind Maps**. He uses visual mapping (which includes but is not limited to Mind Map) as the cornerstone of his learning method, CLM (Concise Learning Method).

Although the primary audience in his book is students, this book is a great resource for anyone who is serious about learning. Here's a Mind Map by Professor Krasnic on the advantage that Mind Map brings to students:

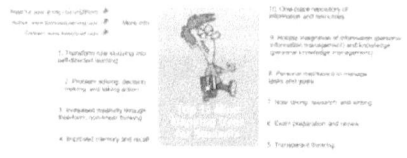

Figure 4-5. Top 10 Mind Mapping uses for students (Copyright © Toni Krasnic)

Group Study

If you are involved in a group study environment, Mind Map can be used to improve the effectiveness of learning dramatically. Everyone has a different understanding of a subject matter, and blind spots can arise if one only considers her version of understanding. Mind Map provides a framework where everyone can communicate and contribute their take on a subject matter to the whole group. As I have mentioned earlier while explaining how to use Mind Map for group brainstorming, you can use Mind Mapping in a group study in one of three ways: individuals complete their own Mind Map then bring those together; everyone participates in creating a group Mind Map; or a combination of the two. If the subject matter is more analytical and clear-cut, such as mathematics or chemistry, the group making a single Mind Map together can be more suitable. If the subject warrants more discussion and exchange of opinions such as literature and philosophy, the group members can find it more effective to lead the discussion based on the Mind Maps they created on their own. Whichever method a group uses, including Mind Map as a tools for organizing and communicating information will help the understanding and retention of the material for the participants, as well as discovery of new and creative ideas.

Presentation

Mind Map is becoming increasingly popular as a tool for presentation. As I have explained earlier on how to create an outline with a Mind Map, it can be used as a means to creating the material and preparing for a presentation. Not only that, but Mind Map itself can be used as the presentation material. People are discovering the benefits of using Mind Map in a presentation because it can present ideas in a more clear, concise and compelling manner. In a more informal setting, some people even choose to use a single Mind Map broken into clusters as the presentation slides. This cuts the time and extra work in preparing a slide from an outline, but you might find this appropriate or not depending on your particular situation. There are several points you need to consider in using Mind Map as a part of a presentation:

Make sure the Mind Map has a purpose and something it's trying to communicate. If it doesn't pass the "so what?" test, it is nothing more than a pretty graphic.

Make the Mind Map visually compelling and easy to understand.

Use multiple colors and symbols when appropriate.

Consider what layout of the Mind Map has the most impact on the viewer.

Problem solving

Problem solving requires a high level of intellectual and cognitive coordination. It requires you to clearly define what the problem is, come up with the possible solutions or alternatives, evaluate the validity and associated risk for each, and then decide on what action to take. Because it requires your mind to be engaged on some serious thinking, Mind Map can surely be of help, just like any other act that involves your mind.

Mind Map can be used in any of the four stages of problem solving that I have just mentioned, namely;

Defining the problem

Brainstorming possible solutions

Evaluate the solutions

• Decision-making

First off, you might start with writing everything you can think about the problem on a Mind Map. Sometimes problem solving is made hard because one does not know exactly what the problem is, or thinks that the problem is something other than it really is. Clearing your head and writing everything down on a piece of paper and organizing the thoughts in a meaningful structure can help you see the problem clearly as well as start thinking about the possible solutions.

When you have a Mind Map of the problem itself, you may or may not create a separate Mind Map to brainstorm some possible solutions. Often you'll get hints of the solutions from the first Mind Map you have created. Then, you can evaluate the solutions on a Mind Map. Here are some points of reference which will help your thinking; the 5W1H (who, when, where, what, why and how), "what if"'s, risks, advantages and disadvantages, the feasibility of the solution, and so on.

Then, you can review all the Mind Maps you have made in the process to make the decision. Not only will the Mind Maps speed up the steps in the process, but also provide a framework for more comprehensive information and reference for you to make a better decision.

Conflict resolution

Conflict resolution is where the problem solving process I have just described is brought to an interpersonal dimension. Problem solving, as I have used the term in the above paragraphs, is a process where an individual or a group is trying to deal with a problem internally; whereas conflict resolution indicates that the problem involves two or more entities. In other words, it is problem solving between two or more individuals or organizations.

Mind Map can prove to be useful when each entity tries to communicate where they are coming from to the other side. Just as one would do in a problem solving situation, you can map out the problem as you understand it. This will help the other side understand the situation on your side, and how you really view the problem. Most conflict arises from the difference in the background and interpretation of a situation. Through Mind Map, you can more clearly communicate your position to the other side. You don't have to bring the Mind Map to the other side and explain each keyword, though it will be very effective; just doing the work yourself will bring more clarity to your own understanding of the situation and make you more effective in communicating it to the other side. If the other side is familiar with the technique of Mind Map, great! You can suggest to the other side that each of you do a Mind Map on the problem and bring it together. It will definitely uncover some hidden issues and hot buttons which otherwise would have left unnoticed. Try this in your personal and professional relationship; you will find yourself become a much more effective communicator and negotiator.

Systematic design

Mind Map is an excellent way to design and portray systems and processes. Mind Map is gaining more popularity in the corporate world, and it is recognized as an important visual tool along with flow charts. In developing a process, you need to figure out all the essential aspects that constitutes that process. You need to know the purpose, the desired outcome, the available resources, and so on. This is where the creative side of Mind Map comes into play. You can address all these issues and make sure you are ready to design a process.

Also, Mind Map can be the end product, a tool for describing the completed system and process. In fact, when used in conjunction with flow charts, Mind Map can be one of the best tools to graphically represent a system, as you can see in the example below.

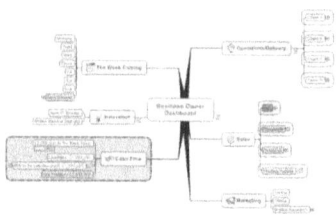

Figure 4-6. Example of a business owner's management system outlined by a Mind Map (Copyright © Liam Hughes)

So far we have discussed some of the potential uses you can apply Mind Map to. I hope that you are now seeing how vast the possibilities with Mind Map can be, and I have barely scratched the surface here. As I have said many times, Mind Map will increase the efficiency and effectiveness of anything you do with your mind. Regardless of your familiarity with the technique, you will find more ways you can use the Mind Map. I hope after reading this book you are starting to reap the benefits of this wonderful thinking tool.

# Chapter 15: How to Increase memory capacity

If you were not blessed with a photographic memory or a type of instant recall that some individuals seem to have, mind mapping can help boost your memory to the levels of those you might envy.

The main ingredient for memory is linking, that is linking the item to be remembered to another item or idea, which is also referred to as association. When your memory has a meaning for what it is trying to remember, it places a label on the item to make it easier to retrieve or looking for it. A related method is reached as you link to some other idea, providing a label for that as well. One analogy is to imagine your memory as an enormous collection of books, each with a label on the spine. Naturally, it is going to be much easier for you to go into the collection and retrieve a memory when it has a label on it.

Using a combination of imagination, association and animation, you will be amazed at how dramatically improved your memory will become in just a short period of time. The best system to encourage imagination and association is mind mapping. It is an effective, creative means of thinking which accurately 'maps' out your brain.

Because they have a natural radiant structure, which begins in the center and uses arched lines, colors, symbols, pictures, words and images, along with a set of guidelines, although you may create your mind map in any way you wish, this brain-friendly tool will help you increase your capacity to remember immediately. Mind maps are simple and not only affect your memory, but will help to improve your ability to concentrate and your creativity. A large amount of boring and dry information can be transformed into an ordered map which the brain will naturally want to follow. By creating a mind map with colorful, imaginative images, text and a spatial flow, you will inspire synergetic thinking as well.

When you begin to enhance your creative skills, you are cultivating a capacity to come up with original and innovative thoughts, ideas and concepts and by default; you are improving your ability to remember more and more. Because memory and creativity are perpendicularly equal mental processes, they each work best when you engage in association and imagination.

Mind Mapping to Improve Memory

When you look at a mind map, you will notice that they only use one or two words per line, a keyword and not a lot of text. This is because you want a meaningful, short word to prompt your memory when creating or reviewing your mind map, not a ton of words.

Mind maps are designed to encourage connections and associations. Creating these connections and associations between ideas and other items is an important link to improving memory. When you are creating your mind map, you are not only boosting the associations between items, but you are laying out the connections clearly as a visual reminder on the page in front of you. By using colors and imagery, mind maps motivate your imagination, which is the secret to an improved memory.

A Useful Tip

Most people know that for something to be committed to memory, you must run through it at least three times. The mind map allows you to quickly review information again and again. Your mind also works by making connections, and mind maps work in this way as well. The mind map helps you to build relationships between things.

If you are using mind maps to study, for example, you can listen to your instructor, write linear notes, and then transfer them to the mind maps. There you go; you have reviewed the information three times. However, you can even take things a step further by reviewing your mind map a time or two before your exam, or you can take it to your study group and expand upon it with them. Furthermore, the fact that the information is put into the simplest form possible helps you to retain the information even more. The fact that the mind map is going to show the relationship between things is going to help you take in and understand the information as well.

Revisit your mind map daily and you will find that the information in the mind map just sticks into your brain. Doing so will also give you a fresh perspective on the things included in your mind map. It will also help you to reconsider things as they change and it will remind you of things that you may have forgotten.

Mind Mapping Example

To take notes using mind maps, you place the main subject you are learning or want to note as the central idea, and then from the center, you branch out with supporting details. This is done by drawing lines out from the center and labeling them with facts or points about the main idea. From there you draw secondary branches that support the primary branches. You expand outward with more and more detail noting information as you think of or come across it.

Here is an example:

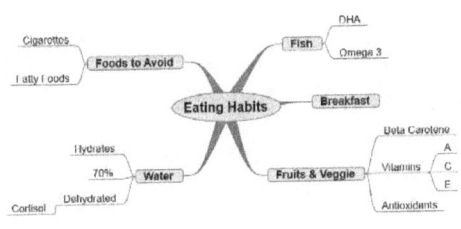

This mind map summarizes the section about eating habits that help to improve memory. Since the topic is on eating habits, we put that in the center.

Within each primary branch, we added supporting facts with secondary branches. For example, under the branch "fruits and veggies," we listed what was mentioned about their benefits, that they are a good source of beta carotene, vitamins A, C, and E, and antioxidants. Under the "water" branch, we noted the important points revealed about drinking water.

So, you start with the main idea in the center, and then you radiate outward with supporting and subsidiary details. There are no limits to the number of supporting and subsidiary branches you create.

Using mind maps for note taking has many benefits. One benefit is that these types of notes are more visual and information presented in visual form is easier to remember. More importantly, notes taken this way help you better structure information making it easier understand. This too aids in memory.

With mind maps, you can do much more than take notes. The tool is great for studying, brainstorming, planning, and writing.

# Chapter 16: Goal Setting And Planning With Mind Maps

When it comes to planning and goal setting, mind maps can help you again. They are a very effective tool to help you get all of your ideas organized and down on paper so that you can clearly see everything that you need to cover and do.

The basic premise of creating a mind map is the same as creating any other mind map, but with a focus on setting goals and planning.

Goal Setting With Mind Maps

Goal setting with mind maps can take one of two approaches.

1) One Page – You create a single page with all your goals on

2) Multiple Pages – You create one page per area of your life you are setting goals in

You start by writing your main goal, or even just the words "My Goals" in the middle of the paper and then you branch out with information about these goals. You can break them into a number of categories like so:

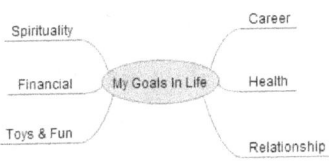

You can then break down these categories even further with sub goals and action points on how you plan to achieve them:

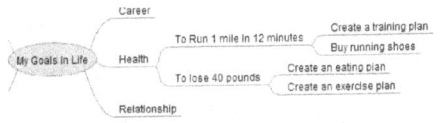

You can break these goals down as much as you need to, which will provide you with a plan of action that you can use to follow and achieve the goal.

When using goal setting for mind maps, pictures and images work very well indeed. These can trigger emotions in your mind, which will help motivate you to achieve your goal.

Think about it, which would motivate you the most to get a new car, the words "a new car" or a picture of the car of your dreams?

The picture would be far more motivating because it is emotive and will fire your passions in a way words won't and can't.

Mind Maps For Project Planning

You can also use mind maps to help you plan out projects. You can use them to plan projects for your business or job, or to plan out projects at home for hobbies or home improvement. The normal principles of mind maps apply and they help to clarify the project and ensure you can focus on all the necessary tasks.

You write the title of your project in the centre of your paper and then you can write out aspects of the project around it, such as Risks, Resources, Timetable, Aims, Scope and any others that you think you need.

Following on from these you can write any other main points you think you need to cover. On the fourth level you can go in to detail about each point

Once you have completed your mind map you will have a picture of the project that allows you to instantly see everything to do with the project. It allows you to 'connect the dots' between different aspects of the project and spot risks or opportunities that you may have otherwise missed.

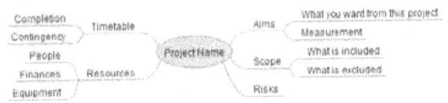

You can see above an example of a very simple project plan in the form of a mind map.

You can go in to as much detail as you need with the mind map and, for larger projects, create mind maps for sub-projects or for project teams that the team can then follow.

Mind maps are an excellent way for you to plan a project and allows for clarity of vision that may only otherwise be achieved with a long and wordy document. It allows anyone to instantly gain an understanding of a project and helps to keep the project team focused on achieving the project goals and deadlines.

# Chapter 17: The Benefits of Using Mind Maps

There are many benefits in using mind maps, no matter where you are in your life or what you do. They are a powerful tool that anyone can tap into and use for their benefit.

Perhaps the biggest benefit of mind maps is that they map the way your brain sees the universe around you and create connections between disparate items. Mind maps help bring clarity to any learning or decision-making process, combining the different functions your brain uses to process information.

When you are mind-mapping, you are using your whole brain to think.

The benefit of a mind map is that you can very quickly and easily see which are the most important ideas by how close they are to the concept at the center and by how it's represented.

The links between concepts can be seen at a glance, allowing your brain to form connections between the different concepts. This helps you review and learn the concepts and their connections very quickly as your brain can recall and visualize it very easily.

A mind map is also very easy to expand upon. You can easily add in more information and concepts as you learn more about the subject. They aren't static at all, being a dynamic form of representing the information you wish to record.

Mind maps form patterns with shapes and colors, which are something your brain is very good at remembering. Even just visualizing the pattern of your mind map can assist with the recall of the information. This visualization helps your brain make connections between the different concepts and different pieces of information that you have recorded, helping you to piece together this information and make leaps of knowledge.

Mind maps have a lot of benefits, even more than the above. As said previously, they are powerful tools that can help you grasp concepts, make decisions, and learn information in a much faster and simpler way than traditional methods. Some of the areas mind maps can benefit you in are the following:

**Learning.** Mind maps help you to feel good about studying and revising. They are excellent in helping boost your confidence in your ability to learn and to study for exams.

**Overviewing.** When learning or problem-solving, being able to take a bird's-eye view of the issues at hand can be very helpful. Mind maps help you to understand the links and connections between the different issues, allowing you to make connections you may not have otherwise made.

**Concentration.** Mind maps help you to focus on the tasks at hands and use all your mental abilities to focus your attention. The mind map itself is designed to attract your attention and to aid in concentration.

**Memorizing.** Using a visual medium helps you to memorize, as most people respond well to visual stimuli. You can "see" your mind map in your mind's eye, which helps with recall.

**Organization.** Mind maps are an excellent way for you to organize information for projects and revision, amongst other things.

**Presentations.** You can use mind maps to help you give a presentation and keep on track and focused on the information you want to present to your audience.

**Brainstorming.** Mind maps are an excellent medium for brainstorming and will allow you to organize your thoughts and ideas in a coherent manner that makes sense after the session has finished.

**Problem-solving.** If you have a problem, then you can present all the information in the form of a mind map and use this to connect the dots between pieces of information. This will allow you to creatively solve problems and find solutions you may not have otherwise seen.

**Thinking**. Sometimes you need to have clarity of thought, and a mind map is an excellent medium for this. You can use mind maps to map out your thoughts and feelings on any subject.

**Summarizing books/seminars**. A lot of people like to summarize books or seminars and mind maps are an excellent way to do this. You can summarize the information and relate points and ideas to each other.

**Planning**. Use mind maps to help you plan a project or event. They can present information and be used to ensure that all processes and eventualities are captured.

There are lots of benefits for using mind maps in your career and your personal life. There are millions of people across the world that regularly use mind maps and benefit from them. You too can reap the benefits of this powerful technique to help you study better, work smarter, and succeed in your life.

# Chapter 18: Listening Skills And Mind Mapping

Listening is an essential skill that you need to learn, because 80 percent of what you know you learned by listening. Mind mapping is a powerful tool in note taking, and it needs to be efficient for students to have a record of lectures for future review and study. Effective listening skills require the constant application of various principles until they become second nature. Here are a few suggestions:

*Be prepared to listen by updating yourself with textbook reading. Be sure to read the topic before the presentation.

*Determine the primary agenda, as well as all the important details associated with it.

*Learn to realize when the speaker is stating an important point by using signal words, or direct statements, writing on the chalkboard, using body language, adding worksheets or class activities, taking more time on a particular area, changing pitch of voice or increasing volume, repeating the textbook, repeating what has been said, giving examples, and pausing.

You can improve your listening skills using the following steps:

*Find an area of interest and focus on it even if the topic sounds boring. You may find some useful information.

*Do not judge the delivery, but rather the content.

*Aim to learn what the speaker knows, rather than how he/she presents it.

*Do not evaluate until the comprehension is complete. Avoid becoming consumed with rebuttal even before the idea has been completely presented. Do not listen defensively.

*Listen out for ideas; i.e. main ideas, organizational patterns, and central facts.

*Resist distractions: This is all about concentration.

*Exercise your mind: Cultivate the habit of watching out for a variety of presentations hard enough to challenge your mental abilities.

*Keep an open mind: Be cautious of the emotional impact of particular words- avoid listening defensively to compose a rebuttal.

*Make the most of thought speed: Ideally, speech speed should be about 100 to 200 words per minute, while thought speed should be about 400 to 500 plus words per minute. Make the most of the discrepancy. Keep off distractions during this time.

Here are some bad listening habits you should avoid:

*Thinking about insignificant topics

*Refusing to accept new ideas

*Avoiding difficult material

*Being distracted easily

*Being poorly attentive to the speaker

*Using inflexible note taking

*Listening for details, as opposed to central ideas

*Allowing excessive emotional involvement

*Judging delivery, as opposed to content

*Finding the subject uninteresting

How to take good notes

One of the most important things you can use while preparing for a test is a good set of lecture notes. If you are equipped with the facts in readable format, you can then do the necessary reviewing. Many students tend to take their notes in a very messy style while claiming that they will copy them later on. This policy is poor for two main reasons: For starters, the notes don't usually get copied, and the original ones are not of much use after a couple of days or weeks. Secondly, if you are copying the notes, this is a waste of time, given the fact that you can do it correctly in the first place.

Use ink as opposed to pencil, as the later will smear and become harder to read. Ensure that you use a large notebook as well, and date your notes for reference. Leave wide margins and avoid crowding your lines together. Furthermore, notebook paper is cheap, so do not mind using an entire line for one work only. Plenty of white space is significant so that you can show how ideas are related to each other. Reduce as many ideas as you can using note taking shorthand. Avoid using complex sentences, but rather essential words only. In addition, use symbols as opposed to words, and abbreviate by using creative spelling, half words, and initials.

# Conclusion

Creating a mind map for creatively and visually addressing problems, increasing your memory, organizing projects and assignments and for better studying takes a little time and some practice. The two hemispheres of your brain are not used to working together and may balk at the thought at first, but don't let that stop you.

Mind mapping is fun and helpful, but it can become somewhat addictive if you are not careful. Do not become caught up in a quest for the perfect mind map because it does not exist. There are no permanent items on a mind map, just as your life moves and changes, so to should your mind map. You should shift items around on your mind maps as you see new and different associations and connections.

Always keep in mind that mind mapping is a tool and not job. Even though your mind map should be colorful and somewhat exciting, it is a functional tool to help you reach a conclusion. If you find you are spending too much time trying to locate the perfect clip art for your mind map or the exact color you desire, stop and start using hand-drawn mind mapping because you are slipping into procrastination-mode.

Keep mind mapping light, stress-free and fun and you will find your life will be calmer, more productive and have a direction and purpose it did not have before you found mind mapping.

www.ingramcontent.com/pod-product-compliance
Lightning Source LLC
Chambersburg PA
CBHW072329080526
44578CB00011B/91